CAMBRIDGE

T0363847

Official Cambridge Exam Preparation

WITHOUT ANSWER KEY

EXAM BOOSTER

FOR B1 PRELIMINARY AND B1 PRELIMINARY FOR SCHOOLS

Second edition

WITH AUDIO

Comprehensive exam practice for students

Helen Chilton, Sheila Dignen and Mark Little

For the revised exams from 2020

Cambridge University Press
www.cambridge.org/elt

Cambridge Assessment English
www.cambridgeenglish.org

Information on this title: www.cambridge.org/9781108682190

© Cambridge University Press and Cambridge Assessment 2020

This publication is in copyright. Subject to statutory exception and to the provisions of relevant collective licensing agreements, no reproduction of any part may take place without the written permission of Cambridge University Press.

First published 2020

20 19 18 17 16 15 14 13

Printed in Malaysia by Vivar Printing

A catalogue record for this publication is available from the British Library

ISBN 978-1-108-68219-0

Additional resources for this publication at www.cambridge.org/b1preliminarybooster

The publishers have no responsibility for the persistence or accuracy of URLs for external or third-party internet websites referred to in this publication, and do not guarantee that any content on such websites is, or will remain, accurate or appropriate. Information regarding prices, travel timetables, and other factual information given in this work is correct at the time of first printing but the publishers do not guarantee the accuracy of such information thereafter.

CONTENTS

MAP OF THE BOOK

Reading 45 minutes	Worksheet 1	Worksheet 2	Worksheet 3
Reading Part 1 p6 3-option multiple choice 5 questions 5 marks	**Daily life** Present simple and present continuous Making questions	**Social interaction** Phrasal verbs (arrangements) Making arrangements	**Hobbies and leisure** Talking about leisure activities Structuring a discussion
Reading Part 2 p12 Matching 5 questions 5 marks	**Health, medicine and exercise** Health vocabulary Opinions and advice	**Free time** Talking about free time activities Present perfect and past simple	**Travel and holidays** Holiday advice Present and past tenses
Reading Part 3 p18 4-option multiple choice 5 questions 5 marks	**Places and buildings** Types of building Asking for and giving directions	**Environment** Environment vocabulary *Will* and *going* to	**Sport** Adjectives + preposition Sports definitions
Reading Part 4 p24 Gapped text 5 questions 5 marks	**Education** Word order Collocations	**Shopping and services** Places in town Matching sentences	**The natural world** Animals Word order of adjectives
Reading Part 5 p30 4-option multiple-choice cloze 6 questions 6 marks	**Entertainment and media** Short reviews Writing a biography	**Transport** Travel definitions Future forms review	**Weather** Extreme weather and environments Conditionals
Reading Part 6 p36 Open cloze 6 questions 6 marks	**People** People definitions Prepositions	**Health, medicine and exercise** Auxiliary verbs Health and fitness vocabulary Giving advice about diet	**Clothes and accessories** Clothes and accessories vocabulary Linking words

Writing 45 minutes	Worksheet 1	Worksheet 2	Worksheet 3
Writing Part 1 p42 Replying to an email (about 100 words) 1 question 20 marks	**Shopping and services** Clothes vocabulary Writing an email	**People and relationships** Relationships vocabulary Parts of an email	**Weather** Strong adjectives and descriptive verbs Conjunctions
Writing Part 2 p48 Article or story (about 100 words) 1 question 20 marks	**Food and drink** Food preparation words Articles, countable and uncountable quantifiers	**Entertainment and media** Features of a story Narrative tenses	**Travel and holidays** Time expressions Phrasal verbs (travel)

Listening 30 minutes	Worksheet 1	Worksheet 2	Worksheet 3
Listening Part 1 p54 3-option multiple choice 7 short monologues/ dialogues 7 marks	**Sport** *Do, go* and *play* Comparatives and superlatives	**Travel and holidays** Airport vocabulary Making comparisons	**The natural world** Landscape vocabulary Adverbs
Listening Part 2 p60 3-option multiple choice 6 short conversations 6 marks / questions	**School life** School vocabulary Linking words Advantages and disadvantages of school	**Leisure activities** Easily confused words Conjunctions Favourite free-time activities	**Sports and games** Sports and games vocabulary Relative pronouns
Listening Part 3 p66 Gap fill 6 questions 6 marks	**Free time** Mixed-tense questions Offers and promises	**Shopping and services** Shopping vocabulary *Have/get* something done	**Health, medicine and exercise** Parts of the body *-ing* and *to* + infinitive Living a healthy life
Listening Part 4 p72 3-option multiple choice 1 long interview 6 marks / questions	**Personal feelings** Adjectives *-ing* or *-ed*	**Daily life** *Used to* and past simple Past and present routines	**City life** Compound nouns Prefixes and suffixes

Speaking 12 minutes	Worksheet 1	Worksheet 2	Worksheet 3
Speaking Part 1 p78 Examiner asks questions 2–3 minutes	**Daily life** Talking about you Family vocabulary	**Work and education** Job skills vocabulary Modals of ability	**Hobbies and leisure** Likes, dislikes and preferences Informal linking phrases
Speaking Part 2 p84 Describing a photo 2–3 minutes	**Transport** Prepositions of place Managing a conversation	**Travel and holidays** Guessing information Expressing interest	**House and home** Home vocabulary Paraphrasing
Speaking Parts 3 and 4 p90 Discussion task with pictures and general conversation 7 minutes	**Shopping** Cause, effect and purpose *Make* and *let*	**Food and drink** Asking for and making suggestions Ordering a meal	**Free time** Discussing opinions *So, such, too* and *enough*

Think about it p96

Exam topic lists p104

For useful information about preparing for the B1 Preliminary and B1 Preliminary for Schools exams, go to:
https://www.cambridgeenglish.org/exams-and-tests/preliminary-for-schools/
https://www.cambridgeenglish.org/exams-and-tests/preliminary/

Daily life

1a Write questions. Use the present simple or present continuous.

1. the sun / shine / at the moment?

....

2. why / you / study / English / this year?

....

3. how often / they / meet / their friends?

....

4. you / look / forward / to / next weekend?

....

5. she / like / watching / films?

....

6. where / your brother / live?

....

1b Now match questions 1–6 in 1a to answers a–f.

a Yes, either at the cinema or at home. ☐

b Yes! I love Saturday and Sunday. ☐

c Because it's fun! ☐

d No, it's cold and wet! ☐

e Every weekend. ☐

f In London. ☐

2 Complete the quiz with the words in the box. Then answer the questions and read the results.

awake	buy	clean	go	go	have	late
leave	morning		routine	wake up	weekend	

Are you a creature of habit?

1. Do you need an alarm clock to help you .... in the morning?
   a) No, I'm usually .... before my alarm goes off.
   b) Yes. Without the alarm, I would just go on sleeping.

2. Do you always .... the same thing for breakfast?
   a) Yes, I don't like making decisions in the .... !
   b) No, that would be boring!

3. Do you ever forget to .... your teeth or brush your hair in the morning?
   a) No, they are part of my morning .... , so I never forget.
   b) Yes, if I'm in a hurry.

4. Do you .... home at the same time every day for work or college?
   a) Yes, I don't like being ....
   b) No, sometimes I'm early and sometimes I'm a bit late.

5. Do you .... shopping on the same day each week?
   a) Yes, and I usually .... the same things each week.
   b) No, it depends what I'm doing each week.

6. Do you usually .... to bed at the same time every night?
   a) Yes, during the week, but not at the .... of course.
   b) No, it depends what I'm doing each day.

Mostly a: You are definitely a creature of habit. You could try relaxing a bit and doing something different for a change.

Mostly b: Your habits and routines aren't completely fixed. It's great to have variety, but remember that routine can help you to be organised.

3

Look at the text in each question. What does it say? Choose the correct letter, A, B or C.

1

> This week's fitness class will be half an hour earlier, at 6.30 p.m., and in the sports hall, not the gym! Next week's class will be back in the gym at the usual time.

A The fitness class will only last for half an hour this week.

B There won't be a fitness class next week.

C The fitness class will be somewhere different this week.

2

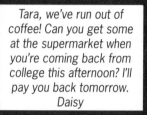

> Tara, we've run out of coffee! Can you get some at the supermarket when you're coming back from college this afternoon? I'll pay you back tomorrow.
> Daisy

What should Tara do?

A buy coffee tomorrow

B go shopping on her way home

C give Daisy some money to go to the supermarket

3

> **BANK OPENING HOURS**
> **Monday – Friday** 9 a.m. to 5 p.m.
> **Saturday** – 9 a.m. to 11 a.m.
> The cash machine outside is in use 24 hours

A You can't go into the bank on Saturday afternoons.

B The cash machine can only be used when the bank is open.

C The bank closes at the same time every day.

4

> Max,
> There's a problem with the shower. You can't use it unless you want a cold one! Someone's coming to fix it this afternoon, so it'll be OK tomorrow.
> Mum

A Someone is mending the shower at the moment.

B It isn't possible to have a hot shower this morning.

C Max will have to take a cold shower tomorrow.

5

> Hi Mia,
> I might be late for the band practice tonight. I usually get the bus, but there are lots of delays this week. ☹ See you later.
> Henry

Why has Henry written the text?

A to warn Mia that he may not be on time

B to remind Mia about delays on the buses

C to ask which bus he should get to band practice

 Exam facts

- In this part, you read five short texts – for example, signs, notices and messages.
- You have to choose the option (A, B or C) that means the same as the short text.

Social interaction

1 Choose the correct words to complete the phrasal verbs.

1. I usually meet *up / out / together* with my friends at the weekend.
2. I'm tired, so I think I'll stay *up / in / into* tonight.
3. Do you want to come *out / over / away* to my house later?
4. My family sometimes eat *out / up / away*. We like pizza restaurants.
5. Who does Max usually hang *up / in / out* with?
6. I was at a party last night and didn't get *back / out / to* until late.
7. We often get *in / out / together* to watch a DVD.
8. Do you fancy going *in / out / up* tonight, maybe to the cinema?

2 Choose the best response.

1. I've bought you a ticket for the concert on Saturday.

   a Thank you. That's very kind of you.
   b Yes, please. That would be lovely.

2. Shall I meet you at the station?

   a It's opposite the bus stop.
   b Yes, good idea.

3. Do you fancy going ice skating on Friday?

   a I'm sorry, I can't. I'm doing something else.
   b Yes, it was great.

4. I'm sorry I'm late.

   a That's OK. No problem.
   b We can wait a bit longer.

5. Why don't we go for a pizza later?

   a No, I don't like it.
   b Great idea!

6. Should I invite Emma to the party?

   a Yes, I'd love to. Thanks.
   b No way! No one gets on with her.

7. Is it OK if my sister comes to the cinema with us?

   a Of course. That's fine.
   b It doesn't matter.

8. Shall we meet up at the weekend?

   a No, sorry, I don't want it.
   b Yes, let's do that.

☑ Exam task

Look at the text in each question. What does it say? Choose the correct letter, A, B or C.

1

Lily,
Thanks for inviting me to your house next Saturday.
I'm afraid I can't come because I'm going camping this
weekend. Maybe we can meet up when I get back?
Sara

Why has Sara sent an email?

A to accept Lily's invitation

B to ask Lily to go camping

C to make an apology to Lily

2

Music festival
15 August
Music includes rock and hip hop
Tickets:
£6 in advance
£8 on the day

A There will only be two types of music at the festival.

B Some performances at the festival cost more than others.

C Tickets are cheaper if you buy them before the festival.

3

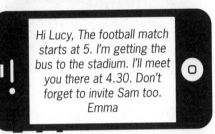

Hi Lucy, The football match
starts at 5. I'm getting the
bus to the stadium. I'll meet
you there at 4.30. Don't
forget to invite Sam too.
Emma

What should Lucy do?

A get the bus to the football match with Emma

B ask Sam if he wants to come to the football match

C meet Emma and Sam at the stadium at 5 o'clock

4

You are invited to a
Jungle party on **June 21** from **3 p.m.**
Dress up in an animal costume if you want to –
a prize for the best one!
Food and drink provided.

A Guests should bring some food and drink.

B Guests must dress up as a type of animal.

C Guests might win something if they wear a costume.

5

Marcus
Don't forget we're going to the cinema this afternoon with
James. I'm not sure what film we're going to see, but we can
decide when we get there.   Jenna

Why has Jenna left a note for Marcus?

A to remind him about an arrangement

B to invite him to the cinema

C to suggest a film which they could see

☑ Exam tips

- Read each short text and think about where and when you might see it.
- Read the options carefully. Don't think an option is correct just because you see the same words in the text.
- The correct answer has the same meaning as the text, but usually uses different words.

Hobbies and leisure

1   Complete the speech bubbles with the words in the box.

club	dancing	festival	galleries	hobby	magazine
member	photography	sightseeing	sunbathing		

Anna — I joined a chess **(1)** .... last year and I really enjoy it now. It's a great **(2)** .... because you have to really think about how to win. You also meet people.

Ilona — I love **(3)** .... to great music. My ideal weekend is going to a music **(4)** .... and seeing lots of new bands.

Ben — I love travel! My favourite activities are going **(5)** .... and visiting museums and art **(6)** ....

Lottie — My ideal leisure activity is **(7)** .... on a beach and reading a fashion **(8)** .... So relaxing!

Karl — I'm quite a creative person. I bought a camera last year and took up **(9)** .... I'm not interested in being a **(10)** .... of a club, though. I'm quite happy to spend time on my own.

2   Complete the dialogue with the phrases in the box.

do you agree that	going back to	like I said	not sure, because
on a completely different subject		that's an interesting point	
what do you think about this		what I mean is	

Sam: (1) ....
museums should be free for people to visit?

Ellie: I'm **(2)** ....
.... they cost a lot of money to run. It seems fair that people should pay
something.

Sam: Yes, but museums shouldn't only be for rich people. **(3)** ....
.... that everyone should be
able to visit them, even if they don't have much money.

Ellie: Yes, **(4)** .... , and I agree with
you in some ways. But **(5)** .... before,
museums are expensive, and we can't expect the government to pay the full cost. **(6)** ....
.... , Ana?

Ana: I'm not sure. I agree that someone has to pay to keep museums open, but **(7)** ....
.... what Sam said, it doesn't seem fair that people who
don't have much money can't see these wonderful objects.

Sam: Thank you, Ana. **(8)** .... , do you
fancy watching a movie later?

☑ Exam task

Look at the text in each question. What does it say? Choose the correct letter, A, B or C.

1

Hi George, I'm going camping next weekend, so can I borrow your tent? You bought one last summer, didn't you? If you've got a small cooker, that would be great, too. Thanks.
Josh

Why has Josh sent this message?

A to ask George to go camping with him next weekend

B to tell George about a new tent he's going to buy

C to ask if George will lend him some camping equipment

2

●●●   **Reply**   **Forward**
To: Photography club members
Subject: Picnic

Everyone welcome – just meet at the park at 2.30 on Saturday. Bring something for the barbecue – drinks provided. Bring your best pictures to share. See you there!
Tom

What should club members do?

A come to the picnic with food to cook

B take lots of photos at the picnic

C tell Tom if they want to go to the picnic

3

Art workshop
Saturdays 10.30 – 12.30
From 15 September for 5 weeks
Suitable for all abilities

A There will be five workshops each week.

B You don't have to be talented to go to the workshops.

C The final workshop is on Saturday 15 September.

4

If you enjoy playing the guitar and hanging out making music, contact us, Neil and Joe. No plans to play as a band – we just relax and play!
Call 07796 245798

Call this number if you want to

A play music with others

B learn the guitar

C join a band

5

Stamp collection for sale
Over 12,000 stamps from a
range of countries
Some antique and rare items
On offer as a collection only,
not as individual items

A The stamps are all very old.

B Some of the stamps are very unusual.

C You can buy just a few of the stamps.

◎ Get it right!

Look at the sentence below. Then try to correct the mistake.

I write to you because last week I started a new English course in the same school.

Health, medicine and exercise

1 Complete the statements with the words in the box.

ambulance	beats	break	dangerous	doctors	fit
heart	injury	medicine	rest	rugby	sick

1. If your .... is healthy, it usually .... around 70 times per minute.
2. According to .... , you should exercise for an hour a day to keep ....
3. Horse-riding is a more .... sport than .... or football.
4. If you .... your arm, you should call an .... to take you to hospital immediately.
5. If you feel .... after eating something, you should go to a pharmacy to get some ....
6. If an .... is painful, you should always .... the part of your body that's hurt.

2 Choose the correct modal verbs to complete the health advice.

1. I'm sorry, you can't see the doctor today. You *have to / mustn't* make an appointment.
2. You *don't have to / shouldn't* eat if you have stomach ache, but it's important to drink.
3. You *needn't / should* worry – it isn't a very serious operation.
4. It's important to rest. You *don't have to / mustn't* do anything for a few days.
5. I think you've got a fever. You *ought to / shouldn't* see a doctor.
6. You *don't have to / should* drink lots if you have a cold or a sore throat.

☑ Exam task

3 The people below all want to join a sports class. On the next page there are descriptions of eight classes. Decide which class would be the most suitable for the following people. For 1–5 write the correct letter A–H.

1 Chloe enjoys team sports but doesn't want to play in competitions. She needs a morning class. She doesn't have much money and can't afford to buy expensive equipment. ☐

2 Mike isn't very fit. He would like to get fitter, but he finds exercise boring. He's looking for an evening class that is different every week. He'd also like to see how he is improving over time. ☐

3 Sofia loves sport but is recovering from a serious injury. She wants to train in the afternoon with someone who understands her injury and can give her advice on exercises she can do at home. ☐

4 Jack is very fit and is planning a challenging 200 km run. He wants to train at least twice a week and would like some personal training too. He wants to train indoors and outdoors. ☐

5 Tara takes sport seriously. She plays hockey and tennis and wants to improve her skills and take part in competitions. She isn't free from Monday to Friday. ☐

Sports classes

A Sport for life

Weekly sessions in seven different sports, including squash, tennis and basketball. Do your favourite sport or try new ones each week. Classes take place on Thursdays 3–4 p.m. and Sundays 2–3.30 p.m. in Green Park and in the Park Gym. We don't believe in winners and losers, just in having fun!

B Top training

Our club offers individual training sessions in the gym, with a personal trainer. The class is ideal for people who enjoy training alone and are keen to improve their fitness, or people who have particular difficulties with their fitness. Classes: every morning 9–11 a.m.

C Active plus!

This is a great class for people who enjoy playing sport with others in an informal way. Choose from a range of sports, including 5-a-side football and hockey. Classes are on Saturdays from 9–11 a.m. We provide balls, hockey sticks, etc. and a monthly report on how your fitness is improving.

D Water-cise!

Have fun and get fit at your local sports centre! Classes every Tuesday and Thursday from 6–8 p.m. No two classes are the same! We organise regular competitions and also offer individual fitness checks every month, plus the chance to gain progress certificates.

E Fitness for all

If you're looking for a gentle, low-cost exercise class, Fitness for all offers exercises to improve your strength and confidence slowly. Our trainers are qualified to help with individual problems and can give you extra ideas to try outside the class. No equipment necessary. Classes: every Tuesday from 2 to 4 p.m.

F Sport for all

This class is for people who want to take up a sport such as football or tennis for the first time. It's a great way to get fit in the fresh air. Classes start with training exercises, followed by a game or small tournament. Classes: every Tuesday and Thursday, 6–8 p.m. All equipment provided.

G Rising stars

We believe sports are for winners! We offer training from professional sports coaches to help you become a more successful player. Choose from a range of team and racket sports. Players are encouraged to join local and national leagues. Classes: every Saturday and Sunday, or book an individual lesson with one of our trainers.

H Go for it!

This is a class for people who want to push themselves so they can compete against other people or themselves! Training takes place every Tuesday, Thursday and Saturday. Classes involve a one-hour run in the park, followed by weight training in the gym. Individual coaching and advice on improving fitness at home are also available.

☑ Exam facts

- In this part, you read descriptions of five people.
- You also read eight texts on the same topic.
- You have to match what each person requires to one of the eight texts.

Free time

1 Complete what the people say with the words in the box.

drama	horror	order	sculptures	stage	videos

Lily "I'm really into **(1)** .... , so I love being in plays. It feels great being up on the **(2)** .... in front of lots of people. I don't want to do it as a job, but it's fun to do in your free time!"

Jamie "I often organise a movie night at the weekend. I invite a few friends and we **(3)** .... a takeaway. My favourite films are **(4)** .... movies, especially really scary ones!"

Rosie "I'm quite creative, so I do a lot of art classes in my free time. I don't like painting, but I love making **(5)** .... out of wood. I also make my own five-minute **(6)** .... , which I put online for friends to watch."

2 Write the questions and answers. Use the present perfect or past simple.

1. **A:** where / you go / on holiday / last year? ....
    B: I went to Spain.

2. **A:** Is Martha still here?
    B: No, she / just / leave ....

3. **A:** Don't forget to order the tickets online.
    B: It's OK. I / already / do / it ....

4. **A:** when / you / move / to this town? ....
    B: It was about two years ago.

☑ Exam task

3 The people below all want to find a new free-time activity. On the next page there are descriptions of eight clubs. Decide which club would be the most suitable for the following people. For 1–5 write the correct letter A–H.

1 Emma loves using her imagination in a creative way. She loves working on projects with other people, and she would like to visit places and see creative people at work. ☐

2 Marco loves making things, and he enjoys meeting people from other cultures. He would like to learn a skill that he can use outside the class. ☐

3 Amina is interested in serious issues. She enjoys listening to talks and learning about life in other countries. She would also like to discuss her ideas and opinions with other people. ☐

4 Niko enjoys going to different places and meeting people from different backgrounds. He's also keen to find out about the place where he lives. He's especially interested in history. ☐

5 Erica is keen to help other people. She enjoys events where there are crowds of people. She wants to learn skills she can use in a job when she finishes her studies. ☐

Activity clubs

A Think!

Do you want to know more about international events? We meet once a week for an informal discussion. Each week we watch a film from around the world and/or invite speakers to help us understand recent events. At our next meeting we are showing a film about earthquake rescue teams.

B Games and chat

We meet once a week to play computer games. We give our views on new games and talk about games past and present. We also organise trips to game shows to see how designers come up with new ideas and create new games. You'll discover a whole new world!

C Party Plus

At Party Plus, we are looking for new people to help us. We organise street parties and concerts to raise money for local charities. It's challenging work, and you have to work with a wide range of people, but you'll have a lot to offer future employers and you'll make a difference!

D Come dine with me

We meet regularly to visit restaurants and enjoy eating delicious food from all over the world. We also invite chefs from other countries to tell us about how food is grown and prepared where they come from. There's usually quite a large group of us, so it's a wonderful way to meet people.

E Nature lovers

Are you interested in nature? Our group has been exploring the wildlife of the city for over 100 years! We organise talks from experts on the animals and plants around us. We also work in small groups to think of ways to improve life for the animals and people in our city!

F Action!

We are a film club, but we don't watch films – we make them! We're always looking for new people with interesting ideas. You will do activities in small groups, so it's a great way to learn new skills and make friends. We also organise regular trips to film studios to see how the professionals do things.

G A world of food

We can teach you to prepare delicious dishes! Our trainers come from five countries, and they love to share their recipes and the history of their cultures. This class will teach you how to create wonderful food in your own kitchen. You never know, you might decide to become a professional chef one day!

H City explorers

Get out and about with City explorers! We explore our own city and produce information guides so that visitors can enjoy it too. We also produce maps of the city, past and present, showing how it's changed. We often get together with groups from other towns and cities to compare information and experiences.

☑ **Exam tips**

- Read the descriptions of the five people quickly and <u>underline</u> the most important information.
- The same information is often written using different words or phrases in the descriptions and the texts.
- Make sure the text you choose matches all the requirements in the person's description.

Travel and holidays

1 **Complete the holiday advice with the words in the box.**

> accommodation   facilities   reservation   resort

I'm going on holiday to Turkey in two weeks and staying at the Bright Sands holiday **(1)** ....
I haven't been before. Any advice?

- I went last year and loved it. It's got great **(2)** .... , especially the swimming pools!
- If you're expecting luxury **(3)** .... , you may be disappointed. But the rooms are all clean.
- If you booked online, check your **(4)** .... before you go. There was a problem with mine.

2 **Complete the email with the correct form of the verbs in brackets. Use the present continuous, past simple or present perfect.**

> ● ● ●   **Reply**   **Forward**
>
> Hi Beth,
> Joe and I **(1)** .... (arrive) in New York three days ago, and we
> **(2)** .... (have) a great time here. We **(3)** ....
> (already / do) quite a lot. Yesterday we **(4)** .... (go) up the Empire State
> Building – amazing! We **(5)** .... (not see) a show on Broadway yet, but
> we've got tickets for tomorrow.
> Abbie

☑ Exam task

3 **The people below all want to go on holiday. On the next page there are descriptions of eight holidays. Decide which holiday would be the most suitable for the following people. For 1–5 write the correct letter A–H.**

1 George wants a holiday with a big group of friends. They are into sports and want to do different things every day. He doesn't like boats, and some in the group have young children. ☐

2 Ana loves to be near the sea. She wants to visit different places, but she also wants to keep away from holiday resorts. She enjoys being active and learning new skills. ☐

3 Harry just wants to relax and have fun by the sea. He loves going out and wants to meet other people. He wants a cheap hotel and would prefer to pay for everything together. ☐

4 Jess wants to travel abroad and learn about a different way of life. She wants to stay with local people, not in hotels. She would also like to see some performances. ☐

5 Greg doesn't like crowded beaches and wants a peaceful holiday where there aren't many people. He enjoys walking in the countryside and is happy to spend some time alone with a good book. ☐

The best holidays

A Golden Sands Beach Club

There's lots to do at the Golden Sands Beach Club in Mallorca. It's a holiday you can afford. Enjoy wonderful beaches and swimming in the Mediterranean or take trips to nearby villages! Then enjoy shows and make friends at the social activities in the evening. All meals and drinks are included in the price!

B Making waves

Our learn-to-sail holiday in Greece will teach you all the basics of sailing. You'll be busy but will still have time to enjoy the silence of the open sea. We stop at a small harbour every night where you can enjoy local food in small restaurants, before sleeping on your boat. Price includes accommodation but not food.

C Forest camp

Get away from it all at Welldale Forest. Stay on a local working farm or in cabins in the forest. Join in farm life or explore the many paths through the forest with our friendly guides. For those who prefer to relax, you can just enjoy time on your own listening to the sounds of the forest.

D Culture shock

Get away from the usual tourist destinations and visit India. On this tour, you'll visit seven cities, see the famous Taj Mahal and enjoy time at a beach resort. You'll stay with families and experience daily life with them. A full programme of cultural events includes some amazing dance shows!

E Seaview Hotel

Enjoy a week at this wonderful, small, luxury hotel in Spain. The price includes all food and drinks, and the facilities include a swimming pool, tennis courts and a restaurant. We organise trips to plays and concerts in the evenings. There's also a beach where you can sit quietly and relax or read!

F Hotel on the sea

Enjoy two weeks of luxury on this cruise around the Mediterranean visiting seven popular destinations. Relax in the sunshine by the ship's swimming pool. You won't get bored, as there are cinemas, tennis courts and a theatre on board, plus plenty of social activities in the evening.

G Active fun

Looking for an active holiday? This wonderful busy holiday resort offers tennis, swimming, golf and lots more. There's something for everyone. Lessons are available, so you can learn something new, whether you're 5 years old or 55! Fun for all the family! Price includes accommodation and breakfast.

H On foot

Do you love walking? Try this walking tour in the mountains of Italy. Each day, you will walk with an experienced guide as part of a group of walkers, then spend the night as guests of local people. It's a great way to see some beautiful countryside and make new friends.

 **Get it right!**

Look at the sentences below and choose the correct one.

Yesterday I've bought some clothes.
Yesterday I bought some clothes.

Places and buildings

1 **Put the letters into the correct order to make words. Then match them to the definitions.**

oiffce	psorin	hlostipa	ctotgae	fcatyor	gtues-hsoue

1. a room or building where people work at desks ....
2. a small hotel that is not very expensive ....
3. a building where people are sent if they have committed a crime ....
4. a building where people go if they are ill ....
5. a building where people make things, often using machines ....
6. a small attractive house in the country ....

2 **Choose the correct words to complete the mini dialogues.**

1. **A:** Excuse me, can you tell me **(1)** *the way to / how far for* the station?

   B: Yes, sure. **(2)** *Take / Turn* left at the traffic lights and you'll see the station **(3)** *in front / by front* of you.

2. **A:** Excuse me, **(4)** *is it far / can you direct* to the museum?

   B: No. Just go **(5)** *straight off / straight on* for about half a kilometre and the museum is **(6)** *on / at* your right.

☑ Exam task

3 **Read the text and the questions below. For each question, choose the correct answer.**

A hotel under the sea

Want to sleep under the sea? The company Planet Ocean has plans for an exciting underwater hotel, which they hope to build in locations all over the world.

The hotel won't be large, with only 12 guest rooms, plus a restaurant. Guests will get to the hotel in a lift – so no diving or getting wet! The hotel will float 10 metres under the ocean, although it will be attached to the sea bed to prevent it from moving too far. Because it won't be very deep under the water, the sun will shine down and provide light. Guests will get great close-up views of the fish and other sea creatures, which won't be bothered by the hotel and so won't make any effort to avoid it.

The hotel's design, with clear plastic walls, means guests will be able to see the sea and all the creatures that live there around, above and below them in their rooms. They will almost get the feeling that they are swimming in the ocean. The luxury rooms will have a shower, TV and even the internet. The restaurant will serve high-

quality meals. As you might expect, Planet Ocean want to encourage people to eat less fish, so guests won't find any on the menu. What's more surprising is that the atmosphere will be silent, so guests will have to imagine the sound of the ocean around them.

The hotel won't be cheap to build and it won't be cheap to stay in. But the designers are especially proud of the fact that it will be environmentally friendly. It will use electricity, of course, but it will produce its own, and won't disturb ocean life at all. In fact, the designers hope some sea creatures will build their homes on parts of the building, which will bring real benefits to the underwater world.

Planet Ocean's future designs include a moving hotel. It perhaps sounds like this will work in the same way as a cruise ship, but this is not the case. In fact, rather than moving between continents and countries, it will stay within a single country's waters, but only occasionally change positions around its coast.

1 What do we learn about the hotel?

    A Guests will have to swim down to get to it.

    B Its lights will shine into the sea so guests can see the fish.

    C It will only have a small number of rooms.

    D Fish and other sea creatures will be scared of it.

2 What might guests find strange about staying at the hotel?

    A swimming from their rooms into the ocean

    B having ocean life in their room

    C enjoying a meal of freshly caught fish

    D being unable to hear the ocean

3 What is the best thing about the hotel, according to the designers?

    A It won't cost much to build.

    B It won't use much electricity.

    C It won't cause any damage to the environment.

    D Fish and other sea creatures won't come very close to it.

4 Planet Ocean's moving hotel will

    A rarely move from one site to another.

    B travel between various countries.

    C be similar to a type of cruise ship.

    D remain close to the coast of each continent.

5 What might a guest in this hotel say?

    A
> It's very expensive, but the facilities are quite basic and the windows are too small to see outside.

    B
> It's great to stay in such a beautiful hotel that is also good for the planet.

    C
> Seeing the fish up close is amazing, but it's a shame that the hotel disturbs sea life.

    D
> It's a great idea, and I love the fact that it can move around and travel to different locations.

☑ **Exam facts**

- In this part, you read a text that includes feelings, attitudes and opinions.
- You have to choose the correct answer (A, B, C or D) for five questions.

Environment

1 Complete the sentences with the words in the box.

| bottle bank | climate | pollution | public transport | recycle | rubbish |

1. I think that .... change is a really serious problem and everyone needs to do more to prevent it.

2. I use .... such as buses and trains. I try to avoid driving because it causes air ....

3. I don't throw paper into the .... bin. I always .... it, to reduce the number of trees that are cut down.

4. I always take glass bottles to the .... It's important to use glass again.

 Exam tips

- The writer may be writing about their own experiences, or about someone or something else.
- The questions ask about the *writer's* feelings and opinions, not what *you* think.
- To find the answer to the last question, you need to read in more than one place in the text.

 Exam task

2 Read the text and the questions below. For each question, choose the correct answer.

The price of a perfect holiday?

Cruises are becoming more and more popular, with around 20 million passengers per year now enjoying holidays on board luxury ships. Many people see a cruise as the perfect way to sit back and do nothing, and enjoy time off work. Everything you could possibly need is within easy reach. On board, there are shops, theatres, cinemas, swimming pools and leisure centres. There are more facilities, in fact, than most towns offer their residents. It's therefore easy to see why they are so popular. But what is the effect on the environment of this trend?

Although it usually takes less energy for a vehicle to move through water than over land, cruise ships are often huge, with the biggest ones carrying up to 6,000 passengers. Moving such large vehicles requires enormous engines, which burn as much as 300,000 litres of fuel a day. One scientist has calculated that cruise ships create as much pollution as 5 million cars going over the same distance. Because they are out at sea, they also burn dirtier fuel that isn't allowed on land. Unfortunately, no government has control over the amount of air pollution out at sea.

Cruises also produce huge amounts of rubbish, and cruise ships aren't usually good at recycling. Waste water from showers and toilets is usually poured directly into the sea – as much per day as from a small town. Waste food from restaurants isn't put into the sea, but still causes problems when brought back to the land.

Cruise ships also cause difficulties in the cities where they stop. Popular destinations can get five or six ships per day, with thousands of tourists at a time. Good for restaurants? No. Restaurant owners complain that the visitors look around for a few hours and then return to their ship to eat. What's more, the crowds can put off other tourists, who complain that the streets are too busy. Some towns have banned cruise ships or put a limit on the number that can stop at the same time. People who care about the environment worry that as the cruise industry continues to grow, so too will the issues for our planet.

1 What is the writer trying to do in paragraph 1?

A persuade people to go on cruise ships

B explain why cruise ships have become so popular

C compare cruise ships with a typical holiday resort

D describe how the services cruise ships offer have changed

2 One reason cruise ships cause a lot of air pollution is because

A they carry large numbers of cars as well as passengers.

B their engines are not as efficient as those of other ships.

C it takes more energy to move through water than over land.

D they use types of fuel that are not permitted on land.

3 What do we learn about the waste products on cruise ships?

A All the waste products are carried back to shore.

B Waste food is often thrown away at sea.

C Most cruise ships recycle their waste products.

D An enormous amount of the waste water isn't recycled.

4 How do some people feel about the cruise ship passengers who visit their cities?

A surprised that they are rude to other tourists

B annoyed that they don't spend money on meals

C happy that they fill up all the restaurants

D pleased to see so many visitors to the city

5 Which best describes large cruise ships?

A
| They seem to offer ideal relaxing holidays, but they aren't environmentally friendly. |

B
| They are becoming very popular and they bring a lot of benefits, in spite of their problems. |

C
| They used to cause a lot of pollution, but things are improving now. |

D
| They cause pollution in the sea and on land, so cities are planning to ban them in the future. |

---

3 **Complete the sentences with the correct form of *will* or *be going to* and the verb in brackets.**

1. Look at those dark clouds. It .... (rain).

2. I hope the concert .... (be) good tonight.

3. That ladder doesn't look very safe. I'm sure she .... (fall).

4. Why don't you borrow Jack's camera? I'm sure he .... (not mind).

5. I haven't done any revision. I just know that I .... (fail) my exam!

6. Are you going into town now? I .... (come) with you, if that's OK.

Sport

1

Choose the correct preposition to follow each adjective.

1. Netball is similar *with / of / to* basketball.
2. You should be ashamed *for / from / of* yourself for cheating in the game!
3. The city of Manchester is famous *of / for / from* its football teams.
4. We were very surprised *at / from / for* the result.
5. Are you interested *for / in / with* keeping fit?
6. Hurry up – I'm tired *of / from / with* waiting for you!
7. I'm not very keen *of / on / for* sport.
8. Who is responsible *for / with / about* organising the event?

 Exam task

2

Read the text and the questions below. For each question, choose the correct answer.

Athletics in Jamaica

Jamaica has produced some of the world's best athletes, including stars such as Usain Bolt and Veronica Campbell-Brown. Is this success partly due to one event – the Jamaica Schools' Championships?

The four-day Championships have taken place every year since 1910. Nearly 200 school students <u>take part</u> in front of an audience of over 30,000 people. The event is also shown on live TV, and the whole country watches what is sometimes called Jamaica's mini-Olympics. The <u>competitors</u> take it very seriously, and they all want to <u>win</u>. Classmates and former students also come to support and encourage their schools.

School <u>coach</u> Dwayne Simpson has <u>trained</u> many young stars. He believes the Championships have an important role in the development of young athletes. They are the biggest schools' <u>competition</u> in the world, he says, and other countries are now looking to copy them. He also believes that the Championships give young athletes a reason to practise. They want to do well for their school, so

they work and train together as a <u>team</u>, so they produce better results.

The Championships have turned many young students into stars, but those who are most talented as adults don't always win as young teenagers. Olympic gold medallist Usain Bolt, for example, failed to win a single race at the Championships as an under-15 runner. Olympic champion Veronica Campbell-Brown was always easily beaten in the lower-age groups before finally winning as an older student.

Nathaniel Day, a young runner from Britain, has studied and trained in Jamaica for the last two years. 'Young athletes here get experience of being on TV from the age of 12,' he says, 'so when they're older, they aren't scared of big occasions and they perform well. In the UK, athletes don't perform in front of the cameras until they're adults, and sometimes they find it hard to deal with.' According to Nathaniel, the Championships also give young athletes a goal. 'Because it's such a big event, it gives them an idea of how exciting it is to perform in an Olympic <u>stadium</u>. It helps them develop the ambition to become champions.'

1 What does the text say about the Championships?

A Thirty thousand people watch them on TV.

B Young athletes take part just to have fun.

C They started over 100 years ago.

D Some former students take part.

2 What does Dwayne Simpson say about the Championships?

A Other countries should try to hold a similar competition.

B They have grown too big in recent years.

C They encourage young athletes to do their best.

D Schools are always keen to do well.

3 In paragraph 4, what does the writer say about Jamaica's Olympic champions?

A They could beat even the oldest students in some races.

B They occasionally lost races, but only to much older students.

C They tried much harder after losing all their races as teenagers.

D They took time to develop into world-class athletes.

4 According to Nathaniel Day, the event

A helps young athletes get used to being filmed.

B is more exciting than the Olympics.

C makes some young athletes feel nervous of big occasions.

D is hard for some young competitors to deal with.

5 Which best describes the Jamaica Schools' Championships?

A
It's an international competition which prepares young athletes for the Olympics.

B
It's an important event which helps young athletes to improve.

C
It's a huge social event which brings people together to have fun.

D
It's a local event which gives young athletes the chance to perform in a relaxed atmosphere.

3 ▶ **Match the <u>underlined</u> words in the text to these definitions.**

1. a group of people who work, train or perform together ....

2. someone who teaches sports skills ....

3. an event where people compete against each other ....

4. join in with an event ....

5. be the best or get the best score in a game or contest ....

6. a large building where sports events take place ....

7. people who compete in a game or event ....

8. taught sports skills to people ....

⊙ Get it right!

Look at the sentences below and choose the correct one.

I'm sure that you will have a great holiday here.

I'm sure that you have a great holiday here.

Education

1 **Put the words into the correct order to make sentences.**

1. favourite / maths / my / subject / is

Maths ....

2. often / Sam / for / appointments / late / is

Sam ....

3. hobby / photography / popular / is / very / a

Photography ....

4. Mrs / usually / us / teaches / Edwards

Mrs ....

5. work / this / enough / isn't / good

This ....

6. Mr Brown / strict / as / Miss Jones / as / isn't

Miss Jones ....

7. too / test / the / for / was / difficult / me

The ....

8. work / checked / my / by / I / a friend / had

I ....

9. finished / we / eating / just / have

We ....

10. film / I / that / yet / seen / haven't

I ....

☑ Exam task

2 **Five sentences have been removed from the text on the next page. For each question, choose the correct answer. There are three extra sentences which you do not need to use.**

A So at least they can enjoy some parts of typical teenage life there.

B That means the school has become a tourist attraction too!

C These young players come here to train, of course.

D During the school day, therefore, they don't go to some of these sessions.

E This has helped it to provide a better education for all its students.

F They are also expected to set a good example to younger students.

G Which is why there are far more of these students than ever before.

H After all, only the best ones go on to join the main team.

Football stars at school

Can you imagine being a famous football star but still attending school? That's what some students at Ashton-on-Mersey School in England do!

The school is about 7 km from Old Trafford, the famous sports stadium that is home to Manchester United Football Club. The club takes talented teenagers from all over the world. **(1)**.......... But even though they are following their dreams of becoming sports stars, football clubs recognise that education should still be an important part of their lives. **(2)**.......... Although footballers can play professionally from the age of 16, most don't join professional teams until they are older.

All football clubs have to make sure that players who are under 18 are getting an education, but many choose to do this by organising classes at the club. At Manchester United, however, young players go to a normal school. **(3)**.......... That's why at Ashton-on-Mersey School you can see people who played against Arsenal or Liverpool on Saturday sitting down to classes with all the other students on Monday morning.

The Manchester United students have classes two days a week and study a range of subjects. While attending, they are encouraged to feel like they are part of the school. They still follow the rules like all the other pupils there. **(4)**..........

There are many benefits to the school from their arrangement with Manchester United. The football club has given money to the school. **(5)**.......... Perhaps more importantly, seeing successful young players in the school can encourage younger students to try hard to do well and achieve their own dreams. Successful players often return to visit the school. When one French-speaking player came back, the students were all keen to ask him questions in French! Chatting to an international football star really helped them improve their language skills.

3 ▶ **Find the words in the text to complete the collocation for each definition.**

1.	going to school	.... school
2.	do what they really want to do	follow their ....
3.	continue to have good football careers	.... to have successful football careers
4.	learn about lots of different subjects	study a .... of different subjects
5.	do what is required by the rules	.... the rules
6.	believe that they belong to the school	.... part of the school
7.	show other people how to behave	.... a good example
8.	give students better lessons and equipment	.... a better education

☑ Exam facts

- In this part of the test, you read a text which had five gaps in it.
- Five sentences have been removed from the text.
- You have to read eight sentences and choose the correct sentence for each gap.
- There are always three extra sentences which you don't need to use.

Shopping and services

1 **Match the descriptions to the places.**

1. You can open an account here.	a charity shop
2. It's often outdoors and you can often find bargains here.	b post office
3. The money you spend here helps other people.	c bank
4. You go here to buy medicines and things for your health.	d department store
5. It might be self-service, or there might be a waiter.	e market
6. You go here to keep fit.	f chemist
7. You go here to send a parcel.	g sports centre
8. You can buy clothes and other things in this big shop.	h restaurant

2 **Match a sentence from Column A with a sentence from Column B.**

Column A	Column B
1. The shop only opened three weeks ago.	a They're comfortable and quite reasonably priced.
2. Customers had always complained about the lack of staff.	b Another is that it has new items on sale every week.
3. Many branches have closed in recent months.	c Or maybe you prefer the popular stores you see on most high streets.
4. I've always liked the clothes they sell.	d So the company recently employed an extra 20 people to deal with this problem.
5. One advantage is that the shop often opens until late.	e She said I could only try on a maximum of four things at a time.
6. Perhaps you only like shopping in small independent shops.	f That's why it still looks so new.
7. A sales assistant stopped me going into the changing room.	g But it was worth it and looked good at the wedding I went to last month.
8. I bought a dress there which was really expensive.	h These changes are probably due to the rise of internet shopping.

☑ Exam tips

• Read the whole text quickly before you choose sentences to fill the gaps.
• Use what comes before and after each gap to help you choose the correct sentence.
• <u>Underline</u> the words and phrases that tell you that your answer is right.

3 Five sentences have been removed from the text below. For each question, choose the correct answer. There are three extra sentences which you do not need to use.

Could a personal shopper help you?

Do you love shopping but can never find clothes that fit you or look nice? Or maybe you hate shopping and just want to get it done quickly? **(1)**.......... They have helped hundreds of customers, both men and women. People of all ages have enjoyed the benefits of their service, and it doesn't have to be expensive. We charge a small amount for your personal shopping appointment. **(2)**.......... So you will probably end up spending no more than if you were shopping alone.

Before you look at any clothes, our personal shopper will discuss with you what you are looking for. It's a good idea to think about money in advance and set a limit on the amount you want to spend. **(3)**.......... All our personal shoppers are trained to know what styles and colours will suit you best. Then comes the enjoyable part! You sit back and relax while your personal shopper looks at the huge choice of clothes in our store and selects items for you to try on. One advantage of having a personal shopper is that you get your own private changing room. **(4)**..........

If you're interested in trying our personal shopping experience, why not come along to one of our stores and talk to us? On days when the store is quiet, one of our personal shoppers might be free to help you there and then. **(5)**.......... That way, you'll be sure you won't be disappointed.

For this month only, if you book an appointment with a personal shopper, we're offering a 10% discount on goods in all our store's departments, including electronic items such as computers and tablets.

So what are you waiting for? Get yourself a new look, and make shopping fun!

A But it's always best to book in advance.

B However, you will get this back if you buy any of the items you try on.

C So the prices are the same whether you use the service or not.

D This means you can take your time, even if the rest of the store is crowded.

E Exchanging your unwanted items in this way makes shopping so much simpler.

F Then perhaps one of our personal shoppers is what you're looking for.

G Because of this, people generally find shopping less enjoyable than before.

H This allows our shopping expert to find clothes within your price range.

The natural world

1 Write the correct animal name for each definition.

bee	camel	cat	cow	dinosaur	dolphin	giraffe	lion	parrot	shark

1. a colourful bird that you can teach to talk ....
2. an African animal that hunts and kills other animals ....
3. a big fish with very large teeth ....
4. a friendly, intelligent animal that lives in the sea ....
5. a large animal that lived a long time ago ....
6. an insect that lives in large groups and makes honey ....
7. an animal with a very long neck ....
8. a farm animal that people keep for its milk ....
9. a small animal with soft fur that people keep as a pet ....
10. an animal used in the desert that doesn't have to drink very often ....

2 Complete the sentences with the adjectives in brackets in the correct order.

1. Lambs are .... animals. (farm, small, white)
2. Their dog is brown with .... spots. (black, round, small)
3. We saw some .... birds. (African, tiny, colourful)
4. Bears are .... animals. (shy, large, wild)
5. The puppy had .... fur. (brown, lovely, soft)
6. We saw a butterfly with .... wings. (shiny, small, blue)

 **Get it right!**

Look at the sentence below, then try to correct the mistake.

I have just bought a new, big lamp for my bedroom.

3 Five sentences have been removed from the text below. For each question, choose the correct answer. There are three extra sentences which you do not need to use.

Bees, bees, bees

Most people enjoy seeing bees in gardens and parks, but it can be scary when they're flying together in large numbers, and it can be even more frightening if they come a bit too close!

A few years ago, Lisa Turnbull was in her home in York. She had made a cake, which she had left on the kitchen table. **(1)**.......... But, as she opened the window to help the cake cool more quickly, she unfortunately didn't notice the large number of bees flying around in her back garden. Lisa left the cake in the kitchen and went upstairs. A few minutes later, she heard a loud noise coming from her kitchen, so she went back downstairs. **(2)**.......... They had left their old home and were looking for a new one. It seems that the queen bee, which controls all the others, had fancied a bit of cake and landed on it. She was followed by 15,000 others!

Lisa calmly closed the kitchen door and called a local beekeeper, who removed the bees from her cake. **(3)**......... Last summer, Jane Norton from Manchester had a similar experience. She was driving home from work when she noticed thousands of insects following her car. **(4)**.......... She stopped the car, hoping that they would continue and leave her in peace. However, they landed on it and stayed there. Feeling rather nervous, Jane used her phone to look online and find the phone number of a local beekeeper. **(5)**.......... It turned out that the queen bee had flown into the boot of the car while Jane was putting shopping into it. When she closed the boot, the queen was stuck inside, so when she drove off, the rest of the bees followed. Jane stayed in her car until the beekeeper had safely removed all the bees – which took over three hours! That's a good excuse for being late home!

A   She realised after a while that they were bees flying after her.

B   There were still a few bees in the room, but the cake had disappeared!

C   She opened the door and saw a huge number of bees.

D   The beekeeper told her that he couldn't remove such a large swarm.

E   She was very much looking forward to having a slice.

F   He arrived just half an hour later.

G   Although it wasn't damaged, Lisa didn't feel very hungry any more!

H   The bees seemed to be attracted by the cake and followed her.

Entertainment and media

1 Complete the reviews with the words in the box.

admission audience classical comedy exhibition
museum orchestra performed plays

What's on this month?

Music in the Park

A concert of **(1)** .... music by Beethoven and Bach. It is **(2)** .... in Central Park

by the Berlin National **(3)** .... Brilliant!

Two's a Crowd

A wonderfully funny **(4)** .... at the Royal Theatre. I saw it last night, and the **(5)** ....

loved it! It's written by James Garland, who has also written several very good, serious **(6)** ....

Animals in Art

A new **(7)** .... of animal paintings, which opens at the Victoria **(8)** .... next

Friday. Well worth a visit. **(9)** .... costs £3, but is free after 4 p.m.

☑ Exam task

2 For each question, choose the correct answer.

Emma Watson

The actress Emma Watson grew up near Oxford in the south of England

and trained as an actress at the Stagecoach School in Oxford.

Although she had only acted in a few school plays, in 2001, she was lucky

enough to get the **(1)** .... of Hermione in the Harry Potter film

(2) .... This was the part which first **(3)** .... her

famous. She appeared in all eight of the Harry Potter films from 2001 to

2011. After the Harry Potter films, Emma **(4)** .... to work in films, but also

(5) .... a few years studying English Literature at university. She acted while she studied,

and since 2012 she has continued to develop her career and has appeared in **(6)** ....

very successful films.

1	**A** title	**B** person	**C** role	**D** hero
2	**A** set	**B** series	**C** group	**D** collection
3	**A** produced	**B** created	**C** caused	**D** made
4	**A** continued	**B** kept	**C** stayed	**D** remained
5	**A** passed	**B** spent	**C** gave	**D** allowed
6	**A** several	**B** plenty	**C** lots	**D** few

3   **Write a short profile of a celebrity. Use the text in Exercise 2 as a model. Include:**

- where the person was born or grew up
- how their career started
- how they became famous
- their main achievements
- what they are doing now

....

....

....

....

....

....

✓ *Exam facts*

- In this part, you read a short text with six spaces in it.
- You have to choose the correct word (A, B, C or D) for each space.

Transport

1 Match the sentences to the transport words.

1.	You sleep here when you travel on a cruise ship.	**a**	return ticket
2.	This big vehicle carries goods on roads.	**b**	petrol station
3.	You look through this when you are driving a car.	**c**	cabin
4.	This allows you to go to a place and back home again.	**d**	hitchhike
5.	You pay this when you travel on a bus or train.	**e**	windscreen
6.	You can travel like this if you don't want to pay.	**f**	motorway
7.	You buy fuel for your car here.	**g**	lorry
8.	You can drive very fast on this.	**h**	fare

2 Choose the correct future verb forms in the speech bubbles.

1. Hurry up – our train *leaves / will leave* at 4.30, and we need to get to the station!

2. I've found a great hotel online. I *book / 'm going to book* it later today.

3. I *'ll travel / 'm travelling* to New York tomorrow – I can't wait!

4. Is your bag heavy? I *'ll carry / carry* it for you.

5. The prices *are probably going / will probably go* up, so I think it's better to book now.

6. The brochure looks amazing – I'm sure you *have / 're going to have* a wonderful holiday!

7. Boarding *starts / is starting* 45 minutes before the flight.

8. I must go and pack my suitcase – I *'m leaving / 'll leave* for the airport in two hours!

3 For each question, choose the correct answer.

Travelling in the Glasgow area

The city of Glasgow has a modern underground rail network and plenty of buses and trains. It also has a few other forms of transport. The ferry **(1)** .... across the river Clyde between Yoker and Renfrew is popular with tourists. There has been a ferry here for around 500 years. The **(2)** .... takes about half an hour and it's an interesting way to see this part of the city. For a longer boat ride, you could try one of the cruises on the Clyde. The cruises **(3)** .... at the Riverside Museum and sail down the river past some interesting historical parts of the city. If you **(4)** .... trying something more adventurous, you could travel to the island of Mull on a seaplane. The **(5)** .... are quite expensive, but it's an experience you won't forget. Or why not try a helicopter flight? It's not cheap, but you get an amazing **(6)** .... of the city.

1	**A** service	**B** delivery	**C** support	**D** approach
2	**A** trip	**B** travel	**C** transport	**D** route
3	**A** leave	**B** depart	**C** start	**D** open
4	**A** fancy	**B** want	**C** hope	**D** plan
5	**A** costs	**B** fees	**C** fares	**D** charges
6	**A** scene	**B** scenery	**C** landscape	**D** view

Exam tips

- Read through the whole text first.
- Look at the words before and after each space.
- Try each option (A, B, C and D) in the space and decide which is correct. If you are not sure, choose the one that sounds the best.

Weather

1 Complete the texts with the words in the box.

| dry | freezing | heat | humid | ice | lightning | showers | thunder |

Extreme weather facts

Antarctica is one of the coldest places on earth, with temperatures below **(1)** .... all year round. The ground is covered in thick **(2)** ...., but there is actually very little new snowfall each year.

Lake Maracaibo in Venezuela is known as one of the storm capitals of the world. You can see **(3)** .... in the sky and hear **(4)** .... on up to 250 days each year!

The Amazonian rainforest is one of the wettest places on earth. It is hot and **(7)** .... for most of the year, with frequent **(8)** .... or longer periods of rain.

The Lut Desert in Iran is one of the hottest places on earth. Very little grows in the extreme **(5)** .... It's also very **(6)** ...., with hardly any rain.

✓ Exam task

2 For each question, choose the correct answer.

Weather forecasts

People have always tried to predict the weather. In the past, people often watched the sky for

(1) .... of how the weather was changing. A red sky at night, for example, suggested that

the **(2)** .... day would be fine. Animals' behaviour also provided information for forecasting

the weather. For example, if cows were lying down it meant it was **(3)** .... to rain. Nowadays,

however, scientists use complicated computer models to produce weather forecasts that are much

more **(4)** .... They can say, for example, if there is a 20% or 30% chance of rain on

a particular day. They can also warn people if a storm is **(5)** .... This is important for

farmers and other people who work outside. It also helps ordinary people know whether they need to

(6) .... an umbrella with them when they go out!

1	**A** marks	**B** notices	**C** signs	**D** alarms
2	**A** last	**B** following	**C** later	**D** other
3	**A** possible	**B** likely	**C** accepted	**D** able
4	**A** accurate	**B** close	**C** true	**D** near
5	**A** reaching	**B** getting	**C** going	**D** approaching
6	**A** bring	**B** fetch	**C** wear	**D** take

3 **Complete the conditional sentences with the correct form of the verbs. Then decide whether each sentence is a zero, first or second conditional. Write *zero*, *first* or *second*.**

1. If we .... (not have) a lot of rain here, the fields wouldn't be so green. ....

2. If lightning .... (hit) a building, it doesn't always damage it. ....

3. They will be OK on the mountain if the weather .... (stay) fine. ....

4. If you see lightning, you usually .... (hear) thunder soon after. ....

5. I .... (be) really scared if I found myself in the middle of a big storm. ....

6. If you don't get too close to the storm, you .... (not be) in danger. ....

7. We .... (go) to the beach if it's sunny. ....

8. I would love to take photos of a storm if I .... (have) a good camera. ....

 *Get it right!*

Look at the sentence below. Then try to correct any mistakes.

If I were you I will go to the countryside because it is a lovely place and it is very peaceful.

People

1a Match the words to the definitions.

1. colleague	**a** the son of your brother or sister
2. cousin	**b** someone who you study with at school or college
3. best friend	**c** your manager at work
4. classmate	**d** your aunt and uncle's child
5. grandparent	**e** someone who gives the lessons at school or college
6. nephew	**f** your mum or dad's mum or dad
7. boss	**g** someone who you work with
8. teacher	**h** the person you're closest to, who's usually not in your family

1b Use prepositions to fill in the gaps in these sentences. Use only ONE word in each gap.

1. The company I work .... employs about 50 people.
2. Stella usually walks .... school, but sometimes she gets the bus there.
3. My older sister is studying medicine .... university.
4. Tony has lots of homework to do .... school this evening, so he can't go out.
5. There's a new student in my class who comes .... Spain.
6. The bus stop is just .... front of the cinema.
7. I feel ill, so I'm staying at home today instead .... going to school.
8. Fiona's often late for school, but she's .... time today.

 Exam facts

- In this part of the test, you read a short text which has six gaps in it.
- You have to put ONE word into each of the six gaps.
- The words you put in the gaps are usually grammatical words, not vocabulary. They may test your knowledge of phrasal verbs or common phrases.

2

For each question, write the correct answer. Write ONE word for each gap.

My big brother

In my blog post today, I want to tell you about my big brother, Steve. He's four years older **(1)** .... me and he's my only brother. I don't have any sisters. We get on well **(2)** .... each other, despite the difference in our ages. He's in his final year **(3)** .... high school and he wants to study languages when he goes to university next year. He's really good at learning new languages. He **(4)** .... already learned to speak three (English, French and German) and wants to learn Russian and Japanese too.

I **(5)** .... miss him when he goes away next year. We often do things together. Last week, for example, we went to the cinema together. The film we both wanted to see wasn't on any more, so we

ended **(6)** .... watching something that wasn't very good. But we had fun together anyway, like we always do.

3

Write a short profile of someone in your family. Use the text in Exercise 2 as a model. Include:

- who the person is and their relationship to you
- what your relationship with them is like
- what they do (school, work, etc.) and what they are good at
- what you do with them when you're together

....

....

....

....

....

....

....

....

Health, medicine and exercise

1a **Complete the short conversations using the correct auxiliary verb.**

1. **A:** When .... you start going running regularly?
   B: About two years ago.

2. **A:** What .... these machines used for?
   B: They measure how fast your heart is beating.

3. **A:** How often .... Helen go swimming these days?
   B: Three or four times a week.

4. **A:** How long .... you had that bike?
   B: About three months.

5. **A:** Where .... football first played?
   B: Some people think it was in the UK, others think it was in China.

6. **A:** When .... you usually have lunch?
   B: At about 1 o'clock.

7. **A:** Unfortunately, two players .... injured during the match.
   B: Oh no!

8. **A:** Keith .... lost a lot of weight recently.
   B: Yes, about 10kg.

1b **Use a word from the box to complete the sentences below.**

diet	blood	patient	temperature
prescription	gym	rest	stress

1. I go to the .... three times a week to do some exercise.

2. It's important to avoid having lots of .... in your life if you can.

3. My doctor gave me a .... and the medicine's making me feel better already.

4. It's amazing how much doctors can find out just by testing a bit of your ....

5. I've improved my .... and now eat things which are much healthier.

6. In my country, doctors only spend about ten minutes with each ....

7. I don't feel well – I've got a high .... and a headache.

8. The doctor told me to get plenty of .... and to drink lots of water.

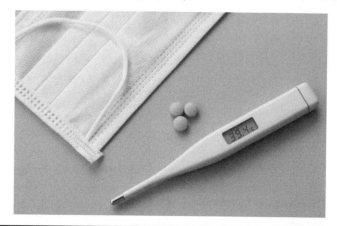

2

For each question, write the correct answer. Write ONE word for each gap.

Getting healthier

I have quite a healthy life these days, but I wasn't always so good! A few months **(1)** ...., I realised that I needed to change my habits. I **(2)** .... spending too much time online and not eating well. I decided to do something **(3)** .... it.

The first thing I changed was my diet. My parents have always provided me with healthy meals, but I often ate unhealthy snacks like crisps and sweets in **(4)** .... meals. I stopped doing this and immediately lost some weight. Then I started to do more exercise. **(5)** .... of sitting at my laptop all evening, I went out for a short run. I ran a little further each week and feel so much better now! I also realised that I wasn't getting **(6)** .... sleep because of staying up late surfing the internet. I've also decided to limit my time online. All this goes to show – anyone can change!

3

What advice would you give someone about eating a healthy diet? Write a paragraph below, giving your ideas.

....

....

....

....

....

....

....

....

☑ **Exam tips**

- Read the whole text quickly before you start writing words in the gaps.
- Then read the text more carefully and decide what kind of word (conjunction, preposition, etc.) goes in each gap.
- Fill in the gaps and then read the text again to check that it makes sense.

Clothes and accessories

1a Choose the correct word to complete the sentences about clothes and accessories.

1. Many women carry their purses and other items in a *backpack / handbag*.
2. I prefer T-shirts with long *sleeves / buttons* that cover up my arms.
3. Sally always carries an *umbrella / uniform* because it rains a lot where she lives.
4. That dress really *suits / matches* you!
5. Billy's shirt *suits / matches* his trousers – they look great together.
6. Why don't you *try on / try out* that dress if you like it so much?
7. Janet would love those shoes – can you remember what *length / size* she is?
8. That shirt *holds / fits* you really well.

1b Use ONE word in each gap to complete the sentences.

1. What you wear for a party depends .... what kind of party it is.
2. I didn't see anything I wanted to buy .... first, but then I found a really nice top.
3. I usually iron my clothes at .... same time as watching TV.
4. I tore a hole in my new T-shirt .... accident.
5. The clothes shop is closed today .... to a lack of staff.
6. My older brother loves fashion and spends at .... £100 a month on clothes.
7. I'm really looking .... to watching the fashion show.
8. My sister doesn't like wearing skirts or dresses and .... do I.

🔘 Get it right!

Look at the sentences below and choose the correct one.

I prefer going shopping with friends to going at my own.

I prefer going shopping with friends to going on my own.

2

For each question, write the correct answer. Write ONE word for each gap.

Making my clothes

I started making some of my own clothes last year and I'm really enjoying it. It was my mum **(1)** .... first got me interested in learning to sew because she makes a lot of her own things. I started off by designing something quite simple – a T-shirt. It wasn't as easy **(2)** .... I thought it would be, and it took me quite a long time. I was pleased **(3)** .... the finished product, though, and I enjoyed sewing it. I liked it so much, **(4)** .... fact, that I decided to study how to make clothes at college. I signed **(5)** .... for a course earlier this year and started in July. So far on the course, I've learned all about making trousers and skirts and we're going to start looking at shirts quite soon. It's great, and I've saved loads **(6)** .... money, as I've bought fewer clothes.

3

Use a linking word from the box to complete the sentences.

but	and	because	so	despite	or

1. The two friends went out without their coats .... the fact it was raining.

2. I could either wear my sandals .... these trainers. Which would be best?

3. They had some really nice trousers, ... I couldn't find any nice shirts.

4. I couldn't get the jumper I wanted .... I didn't have enough money.

5. The weather was really warm, ... Anna decided to wear shorts and a T-shirt.

6. I've bought Mum a necklace for her birthday .... I've also got her a bracelet.

Shopping and services

1 Match the definitions to the words for clothes.

1. They're a kind of jewellery.		**a** collar
2. People wear this on the beach to go in the sea.		**b** belt
3. You wear this under your other clothes.		**c** kit
4. You wear these on your feet, especially in winter.		**d** earrings
5. This is the part of a shirt that goes around your neck.		**e** underwear
6. You might see these on dress or shirt material.		**f** raincoat
7. These keep your hands warm.		**g** boots
8. You might wear this if your trousers are too loose.		**h** swimsuit
9. You might put this on in wet weather.		**i** gloves
10. Footballers wear this to show which team they are playing for.		**j** stripes

2 Read the email. Find:

1. the sentence which says why Josh is writing ....

2. the phrase Josh uses to apologise ....

3. the sentence which explains why he can't go shopping on Saturday ....

4. the sentence which suggests when and where they could meet ....

5. two linking words ....

● ● ●   <u>Reply</u>   <u>Forward</u>

Subject: Shopping trip

Hi Liam,
I'm emailing you about the shopping trip we planned on Saturday. I'm afraid I can't go because I'm going to visit my sister in London. Maybe you could come round to my house on Sunday and we could go into town together then?
Josh

 **Exam task**

3

Read this email from your English-speaking friend Blake and the notes you have made.

● ● ●   **Reply**   **Forward**

From: Blake
Subject: New shopping centre

Hi!

Do you remember we talked about going to that new shopping centre? Well, my brother says he'll take us there this weekend if we want.

Great! ⟶ My brother can go on either day, so which day is better for you? ◀—— Say which day

It's actually my brother's birthday soon, so I'd like to buy him present while we're there – what do you think I should get him?

Suggest ⟶

There's a cinema very near the shopping centre and ice skating too. We could do one of those after we've finished shopping. Which would you prefer? ◀—— Explain to Blake

See you soon

Blake

Write your **email** to Blake, using **all the notes**, in about **100 words**.

....

....

....

....

....

....

....

☑ Exam facts

- In this part of the test, you read an email from someone and some comments about the information in the email.
- You have to reply to the email using the comments.
- You have to use all of the comments and write about 100 words.

People and relationships

1 Read about three problems with relationships. Complete the problems with the correct words.

annoying	arguments	ask	disagree	get on
in common	relationship	respect	share	similar

A I'm going camping with some friends this summer. I've got to share a tent with two other girls, but I really don't **(1)** .... with one of them. We don't have anything **(2)** ...., and I find her really **(3)** .... ! What shall I do?
Edith

B I love my family, but my brother and I **(4)** .... about everything. We often have **(5)** .... and he doesn't **(6)** .... my opinions at all. I'd like to have a better **(7)** .... with him. What can I do?
Adam

C There's a girl that I talk to at the bus stop every morning. We **(8)** .... a lot of interests, and I think we're quite **(9)** .... in a lot of ways. I'd like to **(10)** .... her out, but I'm scared she'll say no. What should I do?
Paul

2 Read part of an email that Emma receives and her reply. Find:

1. an informal phrase that Emma uses to start her email
2. the part of Emma's email that answers her friend's first question
3. the part that answers her friend's second question
4. five short forms that Emma uses to make her email informal
5. five adjectives and one intensifying adverb that Emma uses to make her writing interesting
6. examples of the present simple, present continuous, past simple, *will* and *would*
7. two phrases that Emma uses to make suggestions
8. three linking words that Emma uses
9. an informal phrase that Emma uses to end her email

> I'm spending a year studying in Australia. It's great, but I'm really missing my friends back home. How can I make new friends here? How do you keep in contact with old friends?

● ● ●   <u>Reply</u>   <u>Forward</u>

Subject: RE: Friends

Hi Jodie,
I'm glad you're enjoying Australia. The weather in your photos looks absolutely amazing! I'm sure you'll soon make friends. You love sport, so why don't you join a sports club? That would be a great way to meet people. As soon as you get to know some people, you could organise a barbecue – that would be fun! I've got a few old friends from when I lived in London. We stay in contact online. We send messages and photos to each other, and we try to meet up when we can.
Take care and write soon!
Love,
Emma

 **Exam task**

3 Read this email from your English-speaking friend Rowan and the notes you have made.

●●●   **Reply**   **Forward**

From: Rowan
Subject: Some advice

Hi!

I've had a problem with my family recently and I want to ask your advice.

Oh no!

We had a big family party yesterday, but I had an argument about something really silly with my cousin and we've stopped talking to each other. Has anything like this ever happened to you?

Yes, and...

What do you think I should do to make things better?

Explain to Rowan

Should I wait a bit before I do anything, or should I try to do something straightaway?

Say which

Thanks for your help and see you soon.

Rowan

Write your **email** to Rowan, using **all the notes**, in about **100 words**.

....

....

....

....

....

....

....

 **Exam tips**

- Read the email carefully, especially any questions you are asked.
- Read all four comments about the email and think about what they are asking you to do.
- Make sure you write about all of the comments in your reply.

Weather

1 **Choose the correct words to complete the sentences.**

1. We had an awful holiday – the weather was *amazing / terrible!*

2. The strong winds *blew / moved* our fence down.

3. The snow usually starts to *fall / drop* in January.

4. It was a really *depressed / miserable* wet day!

5. My little sister is *anxious / terrified* of storms.

6. Let's go outside while the sun is *shining / lighting.*

7. We were all *brilliant / delighted* when the sun came out.

8. We've had a lot of rain – I hope the river won't *flow / flood.*

2 **Choose the correct words to complete the text about the weather in Iceland.**

(1) .... it is situated in the far north of Europe, Iceland's climate is not as cold as you might expect. The island **(2)** .... attracts a large number of tourists. From May to September, visitors can enjoy daylight almost 24 hours a day. **(3)** .... , it is often cloudy for at least a part of each day, so don't expect 24-hour sunshine! There are frequent showers **(4)** .... , so it's a good idea to bring a raincoat with you. Winter is the time of long nights and colder weather. There are **(5)** .... frequent storms, which can be frightening. You might think this would stop the tourists from coming, **(6)** ...., in fact, the country is still a popular destination in winter, **(7)** .... of the bad weather. Visitors should bring warm clothing and a swimsuit **(8)** .... if they want to try a swim in one of the country's natural hot swimming pools, such as the famous Blue Lagoon.

1. **A** However	**B** But	**C** Although
2. **A** also	**B** and	**C** as well
3. **A** Despite	**B** However	**C** Although
4. **A** too	**B** also	**C** and
5. **A** also	**B** as well	**C** too
6. **A** and	**B** but	**C** however
7. **A** despite	**B** however	**C** in spite
8. **A** addition	**B** also	**C** as well

☑ Exam task

Read this email from your English-speaking friend Marley and the notes you have made.

● ● ●   **Reply   Forward**

From: Marley
Subject: My holiday

Hi!

I'm going on holiday to your country next month with my family. ← Fantastic!

What's the weather like at that time of year? ← Explain

I'm just planning what I need to take. What sort of clothes do you think I need to take? ← Tell Marley

What do you think I should do while I'm there? ← Suggest

Thanks for your help.

Marley

Write your email to Marley, using all the notes, in about 100 words.

....
....
....
....
....
....
....

◎ Get it right!

Look at the sentences below and choose the correct one.

My mum also said me to take some T-shirts.

My mum also told me to take some T-shirts.

Food and drink

1a Complete the two recipes with the words in the boxes.

add	fresh	fry	onion	roll	serve	spicy	up

A

Cut **(1)** .... some meat and an **(2)** .... into very small pieces. You can do this in a food mixer if you have one. **(3)** .... salt and pepper, and some **(4)** .... herbs and form it into a round, flat shape. Grill this, or **(5)** .... it in hot oil. **(6)** .... it in a bread **(7)** .... , with tomato sauce or a hot, **(8)** .... barbecue sauce.

boil	butter	cook	cover	saucepan	smooth	stir	vegetables

B

Cut onions, carrots and other fresh **(1)** .... into small pieces. Put them into a large **(2)** .... with a small amount of **(3)** .... or oil. **(4)** .... slowly for a few minutes on a low heat, then **(5)** .... with hot water, increase the heat and **(6)** .... for about 45 minutes. Mix everything together in a food mixer until it is completely **(7)** .... **(8)** .... in a little fresh cream and pour into bowls. Serve with bread and butter.

1b Now match each recipe to a description of the dish. There are two descriptions you don't need.

1. a lovely vegetable soup for a tasty winter lunch ....
2. a wonderful dish of meat cooked in a fresh tomato sauce ....
3. a tasty, healthy burger ....
4. a delicious pie made with meat and fresh vegetables ....

2 Choose the correct alternative to complete the sentences.

1. Would you like *a / some* biscuit with your coffee?
2. Stir in the chocolate, then bake *a / the* cake for 45 minutes.
3. I'm a vegetarian, so I don't eat *- / the* meat.
4. *- / The* French fries aren't very healthy.
5. I'm afraid I haven't got *any / some* orange juice.
6. There are *plenty of / much* dishes on the menu to choose from.
7. You don't need to add *much / many* salt.
8. I've got *any / some* fish for dinner.

 **Exam task**

You see this notice on an English-language website.

Articles wanted!
My favourite restaurant

Do you have a favourite restaurant?

What makes it such a good place to eat? Is it the place, the food, the staff or all of these things?

What would make it even better?

Tell us about it!

Write an article answering these questions. We will publish the most interesting ones on our website.

Write your **article** in about **100 words**.

....

....

....

....

....

....

....

....

 **Exam facts**

- In this part of the exam, you can choose from two different tasks.
- The first task is an article and the second task is a story.
- For the article, you read a notice and write an article using the information in the notice.
- For the story, you are given the first line and you must continue the story.
- You need to write about 100 words for both tasks.
- You only need to do ONE of the tasks!

Entertainment and media

1 **Read the story and answer the questions.**

1. Which paragraph deals with the background to the main events?

2. Which paragraph includes the main events of the story?

3. Which paragraph includes a conclusion?

4. Underline two examples of the past continuous, and two examples of the past perfect.

5. Put boxes around three words that are used to order the events in the story.

6. Circle examples of adjectives and adverbs that make the story more interesting and exciting.

My day as a film actor

A
Last summer, a film company was making a film in my town. I had always wanted to be in a film, so I applied to be in a crowd scene. I was delighted when I was chosen!

B
The day of the filming arrived. First, they gave us our costumes. Next, someone did our make-up and hair.
I stood there nervously while I was waiting for my scene.
It had to be perfect! We practised 20 times. Finally, the director was happy and we filmed it.

C
Unfortunately, I didn't become a film star, but I met some famous actors and I had a fantastic day! Three months later, I was very proud to watch the film that I had made!

2 **Choose the correct verb forms to complete the sentences.**

1. I didn't perform well because I *didn't learn / hadn't learned* all my words properly.

2. Daniel Radcliffe *played / was playing* Harry in all the Harry Potter films.

3. She first *appeared / was appearing* on TV as an actor, and later she was given her own chat show.

4. I suddenly lost my voice while I *sang / was singing* on stage.

5. My sister went to drama school because she *had always wanted / was always wanting* to be an actor.

6. I met some famous singers when I *was working / had worked* at a music festival.

7. The star refused to answer when the interviewer *asked / was asking* him about his personal life.

8. Some friends took me to see an exciting new band that they *were hearing / had heard* about.

 **Exam task**

3

Your English teacher has asked you to write a story. Your story must begin with this sentence.

I saw the advert for a talent show and decided to apply.

Write your **story** in about **100 words**.

....
....
....
....
....
....
....
....
....
....
....
....
....
....

 **Exam tips**

If you choose the story:

- Make sure your story begins with the sentence given in the instructions and it has a definite ending.
- Try to use a variety of tenses and structures in your writing.

If you choose the article:

- Make sure you answer all of the questions in the notice when you write your article.
- Make sure your article has a clear introduction and ending.

Travel and holidays

1 Choose the correct time expressions to complete the story.

I woke up early last Saturday morning. I was really excited because I was going to Florida to visit my uncle. I didn't want to forget anything! **(1)** *Then / First*, I packed my bags and checked the weight – no problem! **(2)** *Then / After* I made sure I had my tickets and passport. **(3)** *Before / Next*, I called a taxi to take me to the airport, and **(4)** *later five minutes / five minutes later*, it arrived. Everything was going

perfectly, but then we **(5)** *suddenly / sudden* hit a traffic jam on the road to the airport! **(6)** *In time / By the time* we got to the airport, I was really anxious. I hadn't flown on my own **(7)** *before / first*, and now I was really late. **(8)** *After / Later* I'd gone through the security checks, I only had ten minutes to get to the gate. **(9)** *Earlier / Finally*, I got onto the plane just in time, and was able to sit back and relax, and begin to enjoy my holiday!

2 Read the stories of unlucky travellers. Complete the phrasal verbs with the correct form of the words in the box. You can use the verbs more than once.

check	get	hold	put	set	take

- When I arrived at the hotel, I got my passport out ready to **(1)** .... in at Reception, but I found that it didn't exist – they were still building the hotel!
- Last month, I **(2)** .... off booking my holiday for a few weeks because I was unsure of my plans. When I finally booked, they had **(3)** .... all the prices up!
- I was travelling to Edinburgh by train last year. The train arrived at the platform and I **(4)** .... on. Unfortunately, I fell asleep, and when I finally **(5)** .... off, nine hours later, I was in Aberdeen – 200 km further north!
- I was staying in a hotel last month. On the day I was leaving, I forgot to set my alarm and I **(6)** .... out 15 minutes after the normal departure time. They charged me for an extra day!
- I was flying to New York last summer. The weather had been really nice for weeks, but on the day of my flight there was suddenly a big storm. My flight finally **(7)** .... off 16 hours late!
- A few weeks ago, I was driving to Manchester to meet some old friends for lunch. I **(8)** .... off early, but I was **(9)** .... up in traffic for five hours, so I missed the lunch! Luckily, I still saw my friends!

Exam task

You see this notice on an English-language website.

Articles wanted!

The best holiday I've ever had

Where did you go? What did you do there?

How did you travel?

What made it so special?

Write an article answering these questions. We will publish the most interesting ones on our website.

Write your **article** in about **100 words**.

....

....

....

....

....

....

....

....

Get it right!

Look at the sentence below. Then try to correct the mistake.

He taught me much things which I didn't know before.

Sport

1 **Complete the sentences with the correct form of *do*, *go* or *play*.**

1. Have you ever .... gymnastics?
2. I'm .... tennis with my friends on Saturday.
3. My sister .... horse-riding every weekend. She's the best rider I know.
4. I .... volleyball with friends last night. They're much better than me!
5. Do you .... yoga? I've heard it helps you to relax.
6. We .... swimming in the river last Sunday – it was great.
7. I .... a lot of athletics when I was young.
8. My friend Olly's .... skiing every weekend this winter.

☑ Exam task

2 🔊 Track 1 **For each question, choose the correct answer.**

1 What did the man do at the sports centre yesterday?

 A ☐  B ☐  C ☐

2 Which sport does the woman compete in?

 A ☐  B ☐  C ☐

3 Where will the friends go running this evening?

 A ☐  B ☐  C ☐

4 Which winter sport was Max good at when he was young?

 A ☐  B ☐  C ☐

5 What did the girl lose?

 A ☐  B ☐  C ☐

6 Which sports instructor is the man going to meet today?

 A ☐  B ☐  C ☐

7 What will open at the sports centre soon?

 A ☐ 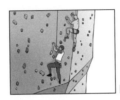 B ☐  C ☐

3

Complete the sentences with the comparative or superlative form of the word in brackets.

1. My uncle's one of .... (strong) people I know.

2. That was .... (challenging) race I've ever competed in.

3. Oliver and Joe can kick the ball hard, but Dan can kick it .... (hard).

4. That was .... (exciting) match I've seen this year.

5. I find boxing .... (tiring) than ice skating, but I'm quite good at both.

6. This year, my coach has arranged a .... (reasonable) training plan than last year.

☑ **Exam facts**

- In this part, you listen to seven conversations or monologues.
- There are seven questions, each with three pictures.
- You have to choose the picture (A, B or C) that matches what the people say.

Travel and holidays

1 Complete the text with the words in the box.

boarding pass	check-in	customs	departure
destination	documents	luggage	security

When you arrive at the airport, you go to the **(1)** .... desk, where they weigh your **(2)** ....

and give you a **(3)** .... so that you can get on the plane. You have to show them your travel

(4) .... , such as a passport and airline ticket. Then you go through **(5)** .... , where your

bags are looked at, to make sure you are not carrying anything dangerous in them. After this, you go to

the **(6)** .... area, where you can have something to eat and drink while you wait for your plane.

When you land at your **(7)** .... , you have to go through **(8)** .... before you leave the

airport, where someone may check your bags to see what you are carrying.

☑ Exam task

2 🔊 Track 2 For each question, choose the correct answer.

1 What time will the flight to Brussels leave?

 A ☐

 B ☐

 C ☐

2 What does the man enjoy most about flying?

 A ☐

 B ☐

 C ☐

3 Where will Maggie's family stay on holiday this year?

 A ☐

 B ☐

 C ☐

4 What has the woman left behind?

 A ☐  B ☐  C ☐

5 What will the weather be like when the plane arrives?

 A ☐  B ☐  C ☐

6 What was damaged during the journey?

 A ☐  B ☐  C ☐

7 Where can you park your car for free?

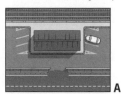 A ☐ 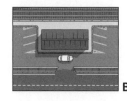 B ☐ 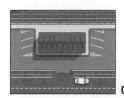 C ☐

3 **Match 1–6 to a–f to make comparative sentences.**

1. The train is not as		**a** expensive hotels in it than that one.
2. Travelling by car is just as		**b** late as it sometimes is.
3. This brochure has much more		**c** is busier than I realised.
4. The tour guide was		**d** boring as going by train.
5. Hong Kong		**e** crowded than the towns.
6. The villages on the coast are less		**f** more interesting than I expected.

 **Exam tips**

- Read the questions very carefully. <u>Underline</u> the most important words in the question.
- The people will talk about what you can see in all three pictures, but only one is correct.
- The first time you listen, choose your answers. The second time you listen, check that your answers are correct.

The natural world

1 **Complete the words to match the definitions.**

1. where a river drops from a high point to a low point w _ _ _ _ _ a _ _
2. the area of land next to the sea c _ _ _ t
3. a very large sea o _ e _ _
4. high rocks, often next to the sea c _ _ f _
5. a low area of land between hills with a river in it v _ _ _ _ y
6. there are seven of these large areas of land in the world c _ n _ _ _ _ _ _ s
7. a large forest in a very wet area r _ _ _ _ _ _ _ s _
8. a hole in the side of a hill or under the ground c _ _ _

2 **Choose the correct adverb.**

1. The rain fell so *heavily / angrily* on the roof that it kept me awake all night!
2. Snow falls so *softly / suddenly* that you can't hear it at all.
3. The sun shines *happily / beautifully* on the hills in the evening.
4. Ben shouted *strongly / loudly* to his friend who was lost in the fog.
5. The wind *lightly / kindly* moved the leaves on the trees.
6. The fox hid *curiously / quietly* in the cave all night.

☑ Exam task

3 🔊 Track 3 **For each question, choose the correct answer.**

1 Which is the girl's favourite photo?

 A ☐    B ☐    C ☐

2 What should people not do?

 A ☐    B ☐    C ☐

3 What has the woman studied in college this week?

 A ☐

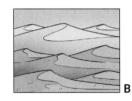 B ☐

 C ☐

4 Where does the man prefer to swim?

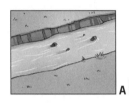 A ☐

 B ☐

 C ☐

5 What did the students enjoy learning about in the lecture today?

 A ☐

 B ☐

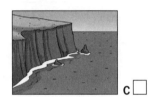 C ☐

6 How did the family travel in Iceland?

 A ☐

 B ☐

 C ☐

7 What did the friends learn about in the TV programme?

 A ☐

 B ☐

 C ☐

◉ Get it right!

Look at the sentence below. Then try to correct the mistake.

It's much more bigger than the old wardrobe.

School life

1 Complete the sentences using the words from the box.

play	talk	uniform	trip	classmates	journey

1. I'm best friends with one of my ....
2. Sometimes a speaker comes to our school to give a .... to the students.
3. My parents are coming to see me in the school .... tonight.
4. I'm glad we don't have to wear a .... at our school.
5. My .... to school is quite long – it takes about 45 minutes.
6. I went on a school .... to a museum last month.

☑ Exam task

2 🔊 Track 4 **For each question, choose the correct answer.**

1 You will hear two friends talking about a school trip to a wildlife park. The boy thinks that wildlife parks

   A help to save many rare animals.

   B are great for teaching people about nature.

   C should just have animals from places with similar climates.

2 You will hear two friends discussing a talk they went to. They agree that

   A the speaker was amusing.

   B the information in the talk was useful.

   C the pictures the speaker showed were interesting.

3 You will hear two friends talking about a new classmate. What does the girl say about their new classmate?

   A She seems quite shy.

   B She works hard in lessons.

   C She reminds her of someone.

4 You will hear two friends talking about a college play they're in. What does the boy want the girl to do?

   A try to get him a part

   B help him learn his lines

   C give him advice about acting

5 You will hear two friends talking about school uniforms. The girl thinks that school uniforms

A make life easier for parents.

B can be confusing for teachers.

C improve students' behaviour.

6 You will hear two friends talking about the journey on a college trip. They agree that

A it was much quicker than they expected.

B there were plenty of refreshments.

C the other passengers were funny.

3a **Complete the sentences using *before*, *while*, *although*, *since*, *plus* or *unless*.**

1. I spend hours trying to learn things for exams, ... I rarely remember what I've read.

2. I can browse the internet for hours .... I realise how long I've been online.

3. Doing homework with friends is good fun, ... you can help each other too.

4. I've made loads of new friends .... I started my new school.

5. I'm planning to go to the cinema this weekend .... I get lots of homework.

6. .... I can see how doing homework benefits me, it's not good to get too much.

3b **What are the advantages and disadvantages of going to school? Write a paragraph with your ideas.**

....

....

....

....

....

....

....

....

☑ **Exam facts**

- In this part of the test, you listen to six short conversations between people that know each other.
- You have to read each question and the three possible answers, A, B and C.
- You have to choose the answer that matches what the speakers say.

Leisure activities

1 **Choose the correct verb to complete the sentences.**

1. Could I *borrow / lend* your tablet this evening, please?

2. Do you and your family *do / make* many activities together in your free time?

3. I don't like *spending / wasting* my free time, so I try and do lots of things.

4. Shall I *bring / take* my new computer game to your house tonight?

5. Don't forget to *tell / say* Anna that we've changed the time that we're meeting.

6. I've *known / met* some really nice people at this concert.

7. Will you *learn / teach* me how to play the guitar one day?

8. Hurry up! We don't want to *lose / miss* the bus to the cinema.

 **Exam task**

2 🔊 Track 5 **For each question, choose the correct answer.**

1 You will hear a girl telling her friend about a boat trip.
How does the girl feel about the boat trip?

   A grateful it was so short

   B surprised the sea was so rough

   C disappointed it was so crowded

2 You will hear a brother and sister talking about cooking.
What is the brother trying to do?

   A improve his sister's confidence at cooking

   B encourage his sister to make him something

   C suggest that his sister should cook for their parents

3 You will hear a girl telling a friend about a band she's in.
The girl says that the singer

   A is very confident on stage.

   B has an interesting singing style.

   C writes unusual songs.

4 You will hear a girl telling her friend about a drama course she's doing.
The girl feels

   A certain she will enjoy it.

   B confident she will do well on it.

   C pleased with the activities so far.

5 You will hear two friends talking about a book they've read.
What did the boy like best about it?

   A It has an unusual main character.

   B There is lots of action in it.

   C The ending is a surprise.

6 You will hear two friends talking about a TV talent show.
What do they think should change about the show?

   A the people who introduce it

   B the people who perform on it

   C the people who comment on the performers

3a **Complete the sentences using *but, though, too, and, because* or *so*.**

1. I practise playing the piano for one hour every day, ... I'm getting quite good.

2. I love playing video games – I don't really enjoy board games ....

3. Max really enjoys cooking and he loves painting ....

4. Emily sees her best friend quite often .... they're classmates and live near each other.

5. I'm going shopping .... seeing my grandparents this weekend.

6. Claire likes pop music .... she hates classical.

3b **What are your favourite free-time activities, and why?**

....

....

....

....

....

....

....

....

☑ **Exam tips**

- Read the questions and the options A, B and C very carefully.
- The people will talk about all three of the options, but only one of them is correct.
- The first time you listen, try to choose the correct answer. Check your answer the second time you listen.

Sports and games

1 Complete the table with the correct words for sports and equipment.

Sport	Equipment
cricket	**(1)** b _ _
tennis	**(2)** r _ _ _ _ _
(3) s _ _ _ _ _ _	boat
football	**(4)** g _ _ _
(5) b _ _ _ _ _ _ _ _ _	hoop
surfing	**(6)** s _ _ _ _ _ _ _ _
(7) b _ _ _ _ _	gloves

☑ Exam task

2 🔊 Track 6 **For each question, choose the correct answer.**

1 You will hear two friends talking about going skiing.
The girl thinks that going skiing is

  A less fun than a beach holiday.

  B too dangerous for her and her family.

  C only exciting for the first few days.

2 You will hear two friends talking about professional football.
They agree that

  A footballers are paid too much.

  B the managers have a difficult job.

  C there should be less shown on TV.

3 You will hear two friends talking about a cycling club.
The boy is

  A suggesting that the girl goes on a ride with him.

  B persuading the girl to join the club.

  C describing where the members usually cycle to.

4 You will hear two friends talking about a sailing course they did.
They enjoyed the course because

  A the equipment was high quality.

  B the instructor gave clear instructions.

  C the conditions were perfect for sailing.

5 You will hear two friends talking about a video game.
They think that it would be better if

    A   there were more levels.

    B   the characters were more interesting.

    C   it had better music.

6 You will hear two friends talking about a basketball game they went to.
Why were they disappointed with it?

    A   The game was boring.

    B   Their favourite team lost.

    C   A player they like got hurt.

3 **Are the relative pronouns in these sentences correct? Correct the ones which are wrong.**

1. Football and cricket are the sports *who* the greatest number of people play around the world.

2. People *what* go cycling are called cyclists.

3. The match *which* was on TV last night was watched by millions of people.

4. *Whom* tracksuit is this? You'll need it for our sports lesson today.

5. People *which* go skiing must be quite brave as it can be dangerous.

6. The referee is the person *that* stops players breaking the rules of the game.

⊙ Get it right!

Look at the two sentences below. Which one is correct?

- The stadium that the match was played can hold 100,000 people.
- The stadium where the match was played can hold 100,000 people.

Free time

1 Put the words into the correct order to make questions.
Then write your answers.

1. go / how / cinema / to / you / the / do / often / ?

....

....

What kind of films do you like to watch?

....

....

2. music / ever / you / festival / been / to / have / a / ?

....

....

What did you enjoy about it?

....

....

3. reading / you / do / enjoy / ?

....

....

What was the last book you read?

....

....

4. exercise / last / you / any / did / weekend / do / ?

....

....

Do you prefer to exercise alone or with other people?

....

....

5. play / musical / you / a / instrument / can / ?

....

....

Which instruments do you like the sound of?

....

....

6. gamer / a / you / are / ?

....

....

Why do you like gaming?

....

....

☑ *Exam task*

🔊 Track 7 **For each question, write the correct answer in the gap. Write one or two words or a number or a date or a time.**

You will hear a film review programme on the radio.

The Film Review Programme

This week's reviews

The film *Jungle Fever* is a **(1)** .... about a family of tigers.

Actor Steve Wills plays a **(2)** .... in his new film, *Call It*.

Swim! is about a man who wants to swim in a local **(3)** ....

Competition for listeners

Listeners can enter an online quiz at www. **(4)** .... .co.uk.

Winners will receive **(5)** .... tickets.

Entries must be received on **(6)** .... by 2 p.m.

Match each sentence 1–6 to the correct response a–f.

1. Come on! We're late!	**a** I'll play with you, then.
2. Please call me when you get to the party.	**b** I will!
3. Are you going to see the Mad Band at the weekend?	**c** I'll get you a new game, if you like.
4. Look! You've spilt coffee on the book you borrowed!	**d** Don't worry – we won't miss the film!
5. I'm not sure what I'd like for my birthday.	**e** Yes. Shall I buy you a ticket?
6. I'll never get better at tennis on my own.	**f** I'm sorry. I won't do it again.

☑ *Exam facts*

- In this part, you listen to one person talking.
- You have to complete six notes using words or numbers you hear.

Shopping and services

1 Choose the correct alternatives. Then ask and answer with your partner.

1. How often do you *buy / spend* something new?

2. Do you enjoy looking at window *displays / shows* when you go shopping? Why? / Why not?

3. Would you rather *pay / spend* your money on clothes or on books and games?

4. Do you prefer shopping in department *markets / stores* or smaller shops? Why?

5. Do you like shopping *alone / yourself* or with friends and family? Why?

6. Do you enjoy buying *gifts / loans* for other people? What do you like about doing this?

2 Complete each sentence with *have* or *get* and the correct form of the verbs in the box. Use one verb twice.

cut	deliver	paint	repair	wash

1. I .... my hair .... about once a month when it gets too long.

2. Hello, I'd like to .... my bike .... The wheel is broken.

3. My grandma .... all her shopping .... to her door now.

4. My parents have just .... the outside of their house .... white.

5. We .... the fence .... after it was damaged in the storm.

6. I never .... my car .... for me – I always do it myself.

3 🔊) Track 8 **For each question, write the correct answer in the gap. Write one or two words or a number or a date or a time.**
You will hear part of a training session for people who are going to work as sales assistants in a large shop.

Training session for new sales assistants
The training manager is called Mandy **(1)** ....
New assistants will work on the **(2)** .... floor.
Part-time workers have a rest day on **(3)** .... every week.
Workers who live in the town can use the store's **(4)** .... service for free.
The staff discount cannot be used to buy **(5)** ....
Assistants need to collect their **(6)** .... on their first day.

☑ **Exam tips**

- You will hear different words or numbers that fit the space, but only one of them will be correct.
- Usually you only have to write one or two words in each space.
- You only need to write words you hear. You don't need to change them.

Health, medicine and exercise

1 Label the parts of the body.

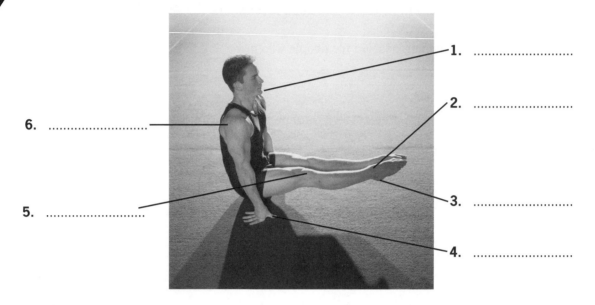

6. ....

5. ....

1. ....

2. ....

3. ....

4. ....

☑ Exam task

2 🔊 Track 9 **For each question, write the correct answer in the gap. Write one or two words or a number or a date or a time.**

You will hear a talk about an exercise class called Extreme Bootcamp.

Extreme Bootcamp

The **(1)** .... use the name 'bootcamp' for soldiers' training.

Extreme Bootcamp takes place on a **(2)** ...., so you can exercise and look at the river.

Members start each class at 6.30 a.m. by doing some **(3)** ....

Wear the same clothes as for other exercise classes, and bring good **(4)** ....

The next bootcamp starts on **(5)** ....

Contact Ellie **(6)** .... for more information.

3a Complete the sentences with the correct form of the verb in brackets. Use *-ing* or *to* + infinitive.

1. Failing .... (take) your tablets on time could cause problems.

2. Many people avoid .... (visit) the dentist because they feel scared!

3. Can I suggest .... (see) the doctor about the headaches you're getting?

4. I'd recommend .... (rest) your ankle for the next week until it mends.

5. I'm hoping .... (get) the results of my X-ray this afternoon.

6. Did you manage .... (pick up) my prescription from the pharmacy?

3b What can people do to live a healthy life? Write a short paragraph with your ideas.

....

....

....

....

....

◎ Get it right!

Look at the sentences below and choose the correct one.

I will spend a few days to go shopping.

I will spend a few days going shopping.

Personal feelings

1a   **Match an adjective from A to the adjective from B which has a similar meaning.**

A

| annoyed | awful | challenging | funny | intelligent |
| miserable | nervous | relaxed | strange | surprised |

B

| amazed | amusing | angry | anxious | calm |
| clever | difficult | terrible | unhappy | unusual |

1b   **Now complete the sentences below with the adjective(s) you think fits best.**

1. I was really .... when Ted said he was getting married – I never expected that!
2. I find maths really .... I'm not very good at it!

☑ Exam task

2   🔊 **Track 10 For each question, choose the correct answer.**
You will hear an interview with a TV actress called Brittany Briers.

1   Brittany realised that she really enjoyed acting when

     A   she played at being an actor at home.
     B   she attended some acting classes.
     C   she took part in a school play.

2   How did Brittany feel before her first theatre performance?

     A   worried about forgetting her lines
     B   anxious that she would use the wrong accent
     C   nervous about appearing in front of a large audience

3   Why did Brittany move into TV acting?

   A   She needed to earn more.

   B   She lost interest in theatre work.

   C   She wanted to try something new.

4   What does Brittany still find difficult about screen acting?

   A   having to repeat scenes

   B   learning to speak more quietly

   C   not having an audience

5   Brittany particularly enjoys

   A   receiving a new part to learn.

   B   attending special events for actors.

   C   seeing her new films for the first time.

6   What does Brittany dislike about being an actor?

   A   not having many holidays

   B   being recognised in the street

   C   starting work early in the morning

3 **Choose the correct adjective, *-ing* or *-ed*, to complete the sentences.**

1. I found the talk on butterflies pretty *boring / bored*. I nearly fell asleep!
2. I'm really *confusing / confused* about what to do – can you help me make a decision?
3. Toni failed her driving test again – she was so *disappointing / disappointed*.
4. Wow! That film was *amazing / amazed*! It was better than I thought it would be.
5. Do you find science *interesting / interested*?
6. I'm so *exciting / excited* – we're going on holiday on Saturday!

☑ ◗ *Exam facts*

- In this part, you listen to one or two people talking.
- You have to choose the correct answer (A, B or C) for six questions.
- Some questions will ask you about the speakers' attitude and opinions.

Daily life

1 Complete the sentences with *used to* + infinitive, or the past simple of the verbs in brackets.

1. My sister Sarah usually goes for a run in the park after school, but yesterday she .... (go) swimming instead.
2. I .... (get up) very early every day when I was a kid.
3. My dad .... (work) for a large company, but now he runs his own business.
4. I didn't .... (watch) the news, but I hate to miss it now.
5. The first thing I did when I .... (pass) my driving test was visit my friend in Scotland.
6. Supermarkets .... (close) on Sundays, but they're open all day now.

 Exam task

2 Track 11 **For each question, choose the correct answer.**

You will hear an interview in which a businesswoman called Carla Smith is talking about her life and work.

1 Why did Carla change the way she worked?
  A She didn't enjoy the work she did.
  B She spent very little time at home.
  C She had health problems.

2 What does Carla say about running her own business?
  A She continues to work a lot of hours.
  B It allows her to take more holidays.
  C She earns more than she used to.

3 What changes has Carla made to her exercise routine?
  A She does more exercise than she used to.
  B She does a new kind of exercise now.
  C She exercises at a different time of day.

4 How does Carla feel about her health and eating habits?
  A guilty about having too many snacks
  B delighted that she has discovered new foods
  C surprised that she now feels so much better

5 Where does Carla spend time with her sisters?
  A in her own home
  B at the cinema
  C at the local pool

6 Which time-saving idea does Carla find efficient?
  A checking emails on the way to work
  B having a lot of similar clothes
  C making lists of jobs to do

3a Put the words into the correct order to make sentences.

1. always / college / for / used to / late / I / be

   ....

2. Zijin / exercise / didn't / at / use to / all

   ....

3. son / teenager / as / my / a / get up / early / use to / didn't

   ....

4. eat / vegetables / Stephanie / used to / never

   ....

5. used to / reply / immediately / emails / you / to

   ....

6. coffee / a lot of / drink / used to / Ahmed

   ....

3b Match sentences 1–6 in 3a to a–f below.

a ☐ but she's very healthy now.

b ☐ but he drinks more water now.

c ☐ but he's in a football team now.

d ☐ but you don't do it as often now.

e ☐ but I make sure I'm on time now.

f ☐ but he gets up at 4 a.m. now!

☑ **Exam tips**

- Before you listen, read the questions and options carefully.
- The questions are in the order of the recording.
- Often you need to understand **when** something happened. Listen carefully to the words the speakers use – are they talking about the past, present or future?

City life

1

Test your knowledge! Complete the compound nouns.

1. There's usually a red one at the top and a green one at the bottom. Sometimes there's an orange one.

   t............................... l...............................

2. This type of transport travels in dark tunnels.

   u............................... t...............................

3. This includes trains and buses. It's used a lot by people who don't have their own car.

   p............................... t...............................

4. You can find out about the attractions in the area you are visiting here.

   t............................... i............................... c...............................

5. Lots of people in cities live in one of these. It has a lot of floors.

   a............................... b...............................

6. This is the middle of a very large town. It's where most of the shops and businesses are.

   c............................... c...............................

☑ Exam task

2

🔊 **Track 12 For each question, choose the correct answer.**

You will hear an interview with an architect called Scott Tenbury.

1. What does Scott say about his 'capsule' apartment in Japan?

   A It was too small for him to feel comfortable in.

   B There was a lot of noise from nearby apartments.

   C He had to think carefully about where to put things.

2. Scott says that the 'upside-down' house he lived in

   A wasn't as exciting as he thought it would be.

   B attracted a lot of interest from tourists.

   C needed repairing regularly.

3. How did Scott feel when he had to leave his home in London?

   A disappointed that it had become so expensive to live in

   B pleased to escape the effects of the weather

   C amazed that so many people wanted to buy it

4. What does Scott enjoy about living in cities?

   A having access to facilities

   B getting interesting jobs

   C seeing lots of people

5 What problem has Scott had with his 'water building'?

    A It's hard to find the right colour for it.
    B It's difficult to build on water.
    C It's not easy to get the right shape.

6 Why would Scott like to design a railway station?

    A to create something people love
    B to test his design skills
    C to improve transport services

3 **Add a prefix or suffix from the box to complete each word in the sentences.**

-ment	un-	dis-	-ship	-ful	im-	-ous	-ation

1. The Eiffel Tower is an ....forgettable monument. It's beautiful!

2. The subway near my house is a bit danger.......... I never go there alone at night.

3. What a wonder........ square to live in!

4. I find it a bit of a ....advantage living so far away from work.

5. You live opposite that enormous depart........ store, don't you?

6. I live next to a big road. It's ....possible to sleep with all the traffic.

7. Excuse me. Could you give me some inform........ about bus times?

8. Friend........ is very important – everyone needs friends.

Get it right!

Look at the sentences below and choose the correct one.

I remember the beautiful beaches where we used to play volleyball.

I remember the beautiful beaches where we were playing volleyball.

Daily life

1 Write the questions and ask a partner.

1. What | your name?

   ....

2. How old | you?

   ....

3. Where | you | live?

   ....

4. Do | you | English at college?

   ....

5. Who | live with?

   ....

☑ Exam task

2a 🔊 Track 13 **Now complete the examiner's questions in Phase 2 of Part 1. Then listen and check.**

1 Who do you .... most time with?

2 What do you .... doing when you're at home?

3 What do you .... about your school or job?

4 What .... you like to do in the future?

5 When did you .... learning English? Do you enjoy it? Why? / Why not?

6 Where did you .... up?

7 What do you like about the town you .... in?

8 Where would you like to live, if you .... the opportunity?

2b In pairs, ask and answer the questions.

3 **Complete the family words. Use the descriptions to help you.**

1. Your _ _ _ s _ _ is your aunt or uncle's son or daughter.

2. If you are _ _ _ _ _ _ d, it means you have a husband or wife.

3. Two people, such as a boyfriend and girlfriend, are known as a _ _ u _ _ _.

4. There are usually several g _ _ _ r _ t _ _ _ _ in one family: younger people and older ones.

5. An _ _ _ _ v _ _ s _ _ _ is the day on which an important event happened in a previous year.

6. Your _ _ p _ _ _ is the son of your brother or sister.

☑ *Exam facts*

- In this part, the examiner asks you questions about yourself.
- The questions are usually about your name, your daily routine, your likes and dislikes, where you study or work, etc.
- You only speak to the examiner. You don't speak to the other student.

To watch videos of the complete B1 Preliminary and B1 Preliminary for Schools Speaking tests, go to: https://keyandpreliminary.cambridgeenglish.org/resources.htm

Work and education

1 Match 1–8 to a–h to make questions about job skills.

1. Do you have good	**a** organised person?
2. Are you a	**b** good at solving problems?
3. How well do you	**c** fast learner?
4. Are you an	**d** communication skills?
5. Do you enjoy	**e** at making decisions?
6. How good are you	**f** working in a team?
7. Do you generally have a	**g** manage your time?
8. Are you	**h** positive attitude?

☑ Exam task

2a 🔊 Track 14 Complete the examiner's questions from Part 1. Then listen and check.

1 Do you study or .... ? What are you studying? / What do you do?

2 Do you like your .... or job? Why? / Why not?

3 What is or was your .... subject at school? What do or did you like most about it?

4 Which .... would you like to learn more about?

5 What do you find .... about learning English?

6 How often do you use English .... of your English classes?

7 If you could have any .... , what would you do and why?

8 What is your greatest study or work .... ?

2b In pairs, ask and answer the questions.

3 Complete the sentences with the correct form of *can* or *be able to*.

1. My daughter .... say the whole alphabet by the time she was three.

2. Which foreign languages .... you speak?

3. Do you think you .... finish the project by tomorrow evening?

4. Jenna has always .... get work, despite not having many qualifications.

5. I .... carry on working – I'm exhausted!

6. My brother .... count until he was six, but he's an accountant now.

☑ **Exam tips**

- For the questions in Phase 1 of Part 1, you can give quite short answers (your name, whether you work or study, what job you do, where you live, etc.) but avoid answering with only one word.
- In Phase 2 of Part 1, answer in more detail; try to give examples or reasons for your answers.
- Listen carefully to the examiner's questions. If you don't understand something, ask them to repeat it.

To watch videos of the complete B1 Preliminary and B1 Preliminary for Schools Speaking tests, go to:
https://keyandpreliminary.cambridgeenglish.org/resources.htm

Hobbies and leisure

1a Match 1–6 to a–f to make sentences about hobbies.

1. I'm not keen on cycling because	**a** since the water's warmer.
2. I don't mind going to the gym, though	**b** it's cheaper than buying them!
3. I love making things because	**c** because they're fun.
4. I prefer team sports to individual ones	**d** it often rains where I live.
5. Although I'm not very good at it, I	**e** it's a bit boring.
6. I'd rather swim indoors than in a lake	**f** quite like dancing.

1b Now complete the sentences so that they are true for you.

1. I'd rather ....

2. I'm not keen on ....

3. I love ....

4. I don't mind ....

☑ Exam task

🔊 Track 15 **Complete the examiner's questions. Then listen and check.**

1 What do you enjoy doing in your .... ?

2 Do you enjoy playing .... ? Which ones?

3 Do you prefer to watch sports rather than .... in them?

4 Do you enjoy .... things with other people?

5 What are the most popular sports or hobbies in your .... ?

6 What .... would you most like to try?

7 Have you ever tried any .... sports? Did you enjoy it?

8 How did you spend last .... ?

2b **In pairs, ask and answer the questions.**

3 **Complete the text with *so, while, after, what's more, at first* and *anyway*.**

Last week, a friend of mine invited me to watch her doing her hobby. **(1)** .... , I was confused: why would she want me to do that? **(2)** .... , I went along to the local theatre, where a band was playing that night. I arrived early, **(3)** .... I sat down and waited. **(4)** .... I was sitting there, my friend appeared on stage with a huge piece of paper, which she stuck to a board. That was strange enough, but **(5)** .... , when the band came on, she took out some paints and brushes as well. As the band played, my friend painted to their music! **(6)** .... they finished playing, my friend showed the picture to the audience. It was amazing!

◎ Get it right!

Look at the sentence below. Then try to correct the mistake.

But it would be better if you can take part too.

To watch videos of the complete B1 Preliminary and B1 Preliminary for Schools Speaking tests, go to:
https://keyandpreliminary.cambridgeenglish.org/resources.htm

Transport

1 **Look at the picture and complete the sentences with an appropriate preposition.**

1. Four people are cycling .... the road.
2. They are in .... of the traffic.
3. The cyclist .... of the others is wearing jeans.
4. The two cyclists behind him are riding .... two taxis.
5. The taxi .... the left is grey.
6. The driver of the grey taxi is looking .... ahead.
7. .... the taxis, there is a van.
8. We can't see any passengers .... the taxis.

2 **Match the questions and sentences 1–6 to the functions a–f.**

1. Do you agree?	**a** interrupting politely
2. What do you think?	**b** asking whether someone has the same opinion
3. Sorry, can I say something?	**c** disagreeing
4. I'm not sure about that.	**d** asking for someone's opinion
5. Sorry, I'm not sure what you mean.	**e** agreeing
6. Exactly!	**f** asking for meaning to be made clear

✓ Exam task

3a Work in pairs. One person is A and one person is B.

🔊 Track 16 **Listen to the examiner explaining the first part of the Part 2 task.**
A, complete the first part of the task.

Photograph 1

3b 🔊 Track 17 **Now listen to the examiner explaining the second part of the Part 2 task.**
B, complete the second part of the task.

Photograph 2

✓ Exam facts

- In Part 2, the examiner gives each of you a large colour photo.
- You have to describe what is happening in your photo and what else you can see.
- You each need to talk for about one minute.

Travel and holidays

1 Look at the pictures of items you take on holiday. What do you think they are? Tell your partner. Use the phrases in the box.

| It could / may / might be … It looks as if … It looks like … It's possible … It seems … |

a

b

c

d

PX092

PASSENGER NAME
SMITH, JONATHAN

SEAT N°   DEPARTURE TIME
27G 19:10

EC.CLASS
006247859
BERLIN

e

f

2 Respond to the information in 1–8. Use the phrases in the box.

| Are (you)? | Did (you)? | I see. | Is he / she? | Is that right? |
| No way! | Oh, really? | Oh, yeah? | That's (amazing)! | Wow! |

1. My uncle's climbed Mount Everest.
2. I travelled around Japan by train last year.
3. My family always goes to the beach in summer.
4. I'm going on a camping trip to the jungle next month.
5. My friend goes on extreme sports holidays every winter.
6. My brother's planning to travel around the world in a year.
7. I couldn't ride a bike because I broke my leg.
8. My sister's won a prize for one of her paintings.

3a Work in pairs. One person is A and one person is B.

🔊 Track 18 Listen to the examiner explaining the first part of the Part 2 task.

A, complete the first part of the task.

Photograph 1

3b 🔊 Track 19 Now listen to the examiner explaining the second part of the Part 2 task.

B, complete the second part of the task.

Photograph 2

☑ **Exam tips**

- In Part 2, describe who you can see, where they are and what they are doing. You can also describe the clothes they are wearing. This includes other people you can see in the background. Then describe other things in the background – for example, landscapes, buildings, vehicles, etc.
- Make sure you know how to describe position – for example, *on the left, on the right, at the top, at the bottom, above, below, etc.*
- If you don't know the word for something in the picture, don't worry. You can try to explain what it is using words you do know. You can also spend more time describing other things in the photo that you find easier to talk about.

House and home

1 Match the words in the box to items a–i in the house. What do you use them for?

basin
cooker
balcony
garage
gate
lamp
mirror
bookcase
stairs

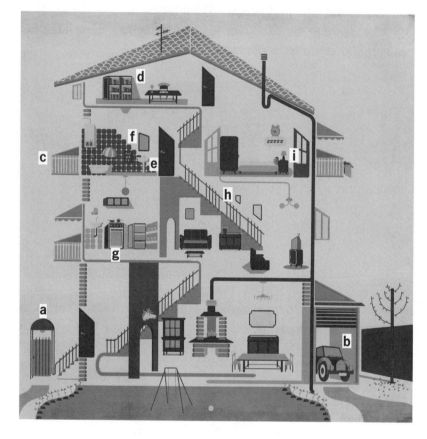

2 Match 1–8 to a–h to complete the expressions.

1. I don't know what	**a** for the thing that …
2. I can't remember the word	**b** what I mean, it …
3. What do you	**c** call it … ?
4. I can't find the word I'm	**d** it's called!
5. I'm not sure this	**e** is the right word, but …
6. What I	**f** looking for.
7. What's the	**g** mean is …
8. You know	**h** name of the thing that …

 **Exam task**

3a Work in pairs. One person is A and one person is B.

Track 20 **Listen to the examiner explaining the first part of the Part 2 task.**

A, complete the first part of the task.

Photograph 1

3b Track 21 **Now listen to the examiner explaining the second part of the Part 2 task.**

B, complete the second part of the task.

Photograph 2

 **Get it right!**

Look at the sentences below. Then try to correct the mistake in each one.

I didn't know that this city would so interesting.

It would be nice see *The Merchant of Venice* with Al Pacino.

Shopping

1 Complete the dialogue with the words in the box. There may be more than one correct answer for each space.

as	because	could	don't	would	should	since	so

Sam: Let's make a shopping list for our barbecue party on Saturday.

Carly: OK. I think we **(1)** .... get sausages **(2)** .... everyone loves them!

Sam: Mm, but I **(3)** .... think we should buy too many burgers – there were a lot left after our last party.

Carly: True. We **(4)** .... get some fish **(5)** .... not everyone eats meat.

Sam: Yes, and how about getting some tasty vegetables?

Carly: That **(6)** .... be a good idea. And the children like chicken, **(7)** .... let's get some of that.

Sam: Great, and **(8)** .... your parents like jacket potatoes, why don't we cook some of those as well?

Carly: Perfect!

2a Look at the words in bold in these sentences.

Let's buy Dad some new boots. Walking in the hills **makes** him feel relaxed!

Which word … ?

a shows that something / someone causes another thing to happen

b is used to make a suggestion

2b Now rewrite the sentences so they mean the same, using *Let's* or the correct form of *make*.

1. I was late for the concert because there was a traffic jam.
    The traffic jam ....

2. Why don't we go to that new bookshop in town this afternoon?
    ....

3. How about going to see the new James Bond film?
    ....

4. We were told we had to run 5 km by our basketball coach.
    Our basketball coach ....

☑ Exam task

🔊 **Track 22** Listen to the examiner explaining the task for Part 3. Then talk with a partner for about two minutes.

Presents for a 16-year-old friend

🔊 **Track 23 Now listen to the examiner asking the questions for the Part 4 task. Pause the recording after each question. Work in pairs and discuss your answers to each of the examiner's questions together. Try to say as much as you can in answer to each question.**

☑ Exam facts

- In Part 3, the examiner describes a situation to you and shows you some pictures.
- You have to discuss your views and opinions with the other student.
- You will need to make suggestions and reply to the suggestions that the other student makes.
- In Part 4, the examiner will ask you questions about a similar topic to Part 3.
- These questions are mainly about your opinions and experience related to the Part 3 topic.
- The examiner may ask you the questions individually or encourage you to discuss the answers together.

Food and drink

1 Complete the dialogues with words from the box. Then, in pairs, ask and answer.

about	don't	fancy	have	shall	would

1. **A:** What .... we have for lunch?

   B: I think we …

2. **A:** How .... getting a takeaway later?

   B: No, …

3. **A:** Which traditional dish from your country .... you recommend trying?

   B: You should …

4. **A:** Why .... we cook dinner for our friends on Saturday?

   B: That's …

5. **A:** Let's .... a barbecue tonight!

   B: I'd rather …

6. **A:** Do you .... going to that new pizza restaurant this evening?

   B: Why don't we …?

2 Complete the dialogue. Then, in pairs, take turns to be the waiter and the customer.

Customer: Hello. **(1)** (*Ask for a table.*) ....

....

Waiter: Of course. Follow me. Here you are.

Customer: Thank you. **(2)** (*Ask to see the menu.*) ....

....

Waiter: Here it is. Can I get you anything to drink while you decide?

Customer: **(3)** (*Ask for two drinks, one for you and one for your friend.*)

....

Waiter: Are you ready to order?

Customer: Yes. **(4)** (*Ask for two dishes, one for you and one for your friend.*)

....

Waiter: Is everything OK with your meal?

Customer: **(5)** (*Say one dish is fine, but make a complaint about the other.*)

....

Waiter: Would you like any desserts or coffee?

Customer: **(6)** (*Say no and ask for the bill.*) ....

....

Waiter: Certainly. How would you like to pay?

Customer: **(7)** (*Tell the waiter how you would like to pay.*) ....

....

3 ◄)) **Track 24** Listen to the examiner explaining the task for Part 3. Then talk with a partner for about two minutes.

Types of food for a student party

4 ◄)) **Track 25 Now listen to the examiner asking the questions for the Part 4 task. Pause the recording after each question. Work in pairs and discuss your answers to each of the examiner's questions together. Try to say as much as you can in answer to each question.**

☑ **Exam tips**

- In Part 3, show interest in what the other student is saying and respond to what they say.
- Look at the other student during the discussion, **not** the examiner.
- At the end of the discussion for Part 3, you should agree on a final decision with the other student.
- In Part 4, try not to give very short answers to the examiner's questions.
- Discuss the answers to the Part 4 questions with your partner, if possible.
- If you don't understand one of the questions, ask the examiner to repeat it.

Free time

1 Respond to statements 1–7. Use the phrases in the box.

I agree that …	I believe …	I feel that …	I guess …
I have no doubt that …	I'm absolutely certain that …	I'm (not) sure that …	
In my opinion …	Personally, I (don't) think that …	To be honest …	

1. Doing dangerous activities like motor-racing isn't very responsible.

   ....

2. Dancing's one of the most sociable activities there is.

   ....

3. If you keep your body fit, your mind will be healthy too.

   ....

4. It's really important to do activities apart from work or study.

   ....

5. Hanging out with friends is as important as having hobbies.

   ....

6. It's important to spend some time each week just doing nothing.

   ....

7. Playing computer games or watching TV is a waste of time.

   ....

2 Choose the correct alternative.

1. I don't want to swim outdoors today because it's *too / enough* cold.

2. Wow! That was *so / such* a good film!

3. Jenny collects action figures – she's got *so / such* many now that she's got nowhere to put them.

4. I never seem to have *too / enough* free time.

5. Adam plays the guitar *so / such* well – he should be a professional musician.

6. I'm *too / enough* busy to go out tonight.

3 🔊 **Track 26** Listen to the examiner explaining the task for Part 3. Then talk with a partner for about two minutes.

Activities for a weekend away

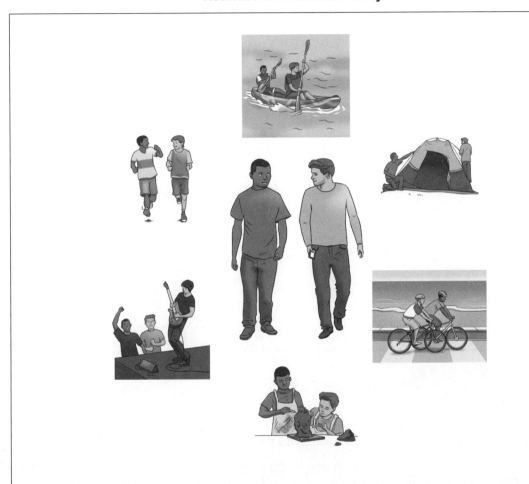

4 🔊 **Track 27 Now listen to the examiner asking the questions for the Part 4 task. Pause the recording after each question. Work in pairs and discuss your answers to each of the examiner's questions together. Try to say as much as you can in answer to each question.**

🎯 **Get it right!**

Look at the sentences below and choose the correct one.

They are such pleasant people.

They are so pleasant people.

 **Think about it** Reading Part 1

Read the sentences about Reading Part 1. Are the sentences TRUE or FALSE?

1. In this part of the exam, you have to read short notices, signs and messages and choose the correct meaning. ....

2. The texts you read will all be the same kind of text. ....

3. There are five texts and no example. ....

4. There are three possible answers to choose from for each text. ....

5. Sometimes there is a question before the three options, sometimes the three options complete the sentence and sometimes there are just the three options. ....

6. There is visual information, such as a picture, with every text. ....

7. To understand the meaning, it is important to think about the situation in which each text would appear, e.g. as a notice on a wall, or as an email. ....

8. It is also important to think about the purpose of the text, e.g. who it is for and why someone has written it. ....

Think about it Reading Part 2

Read the information about Reading Part 2. Complete the information with the words in the box.

| all | eight | five | match | people | points | suitable | text |

In Part 2, you have to **(1)** .... people to different products, places or activities. There are **(2)** .... short descriptions of people, saying what they each want, need or are interested in. There are **(3)** .... descriptions of products, places or activities, so there are three that you don't need to match. It's a good idea to read the descriptions of the **(4)** .... first and note what each one is looking for. Each person will mention three key **(5)** .... that they are looking for. Then you can read the descriptions of the products, places or activities and find the one that is the most **(6)** .... for each person. Some points are mentioned in more than one **(7)** .... , but it's important to find the text that mentions **(8)** .... the key points a person is looking for.

 **Think about it** Reading Part 3

Read the sentences about Reading Part 3. Choose the correct words to complete the sentences.

1. There are .... multiple-choice questions. (five / ten)

2. There are .... options for each question. (three / four)

3. To answer the questions, you need to understand the writer's .... and attitude, as well as the information in the text. (opinion / background)

4. One of the questions is occasionally about the writer's .... in writing a paragraph. (history / purpose)

5. The final question always asks about the .... meaning of the text. (global / detailed)

6. The first four questions might ask about .... information in the text or about the writer's feelings. (general / detailed)

7. The first four questions usually follow the .... of the information in the text. (order / meaning)

8. You need to find the answer for the .... question in several different paragraphs in the text. (first / last)

 **Think about it** Reading Part 4

Read the sentences about Reading Part 4. Choose the correct words in the brackets to complete the sentences.

1. In Part 4, you have to read a *longer / shorter* text.

2. There *might be some / won't be any* unfamiliar vocabulary in the text.

3. The questions are in the form of *five / ten* sentences that have been removed from the text.

4. You need to understand the meaning and *structure / title* of the text to decide where the sentences go.

5. You *have to / don't have to* understand every single word of the text.

6. There are also *three / five* extra sentences that do not fit anywhere in the text.

7. It's important to read the information *before / after / before and after* each gap before choosing an answer.

8. It's a good idea to read the text quickly *before / after / before and after* you choose your answers.

 **Think about it** Reading Part 5

Read the sentences about Reading Part 5. Which TWO sentences are false?

1. Part 5 is a short text with six gaps.

2. For each gap, there are four possible words to choose from.

3. For some gaps, there is more than one correct answer.

4. This part of the exam tests your vocabulary.

5. It's a good idea to read the whole text first, before you choose the correct answers.

6. The options often have similar meanings, so you need to think about how the words are used in a sentence, as well as their meanings.

7. The text may contain some high-level vocabulary.

8. It's a good idea to read the text through when you have finished to see if it makes sense with the options you have chosen.

 **Think about it** Reading Part 6

Use a word from the box to complete the sentences about Reading Part 6.

| six | different | prepositions | sense | overall | grammar | blogs | one |

1. Part 6 is a short text with .... gaps.

2. You must put .... word into each gap.

3. This part of the test checks your knowledge of ....

4. The missing words may be .... , articles, auxiliary and modal verbs, pronouns, etc.

5. The texts might be short articles, ... , reports, emails, etc.

6. Each gap needs a .... word, so you should never have the same word in more than one gap.

7. It's a good idea to read the text through before you start to get an understanding of the .... meaning.

8. It's also a good idea to read the text through when you have finished to see if it makes ....

 **Writing Part 1**

Read the sentences about Writing Part 1. Are the sentences TRUE or FALSE? Correct the false sentences.

1. In this task, you have to reply to an email. ....

   ....

2. There are five comments that refer to what's in the email. ....

   ....

3. You must use all of the comments in your reply. ....

   ....

4. You can write a paragraph about each of the comments. ....

   ....

5. You must write about 150 words. ....

   ....

6. You should organise your writing so it looks like a proper reply. ....

   ....

7. If you don't respond to one or more of the comments, you will get a lower mark. ....

   ....

8. You should put your name at the bottom of your reply. ....

   ....

 **Writing Part 2**

Read the information about Writing Part 2. Choose the correct words to complete the information.

In Part 2, you have to write about **(1)** *80 / 100* words. You can choose between writing an article or a **(2)** *story / report*. For the article, you read information in a notice or announcement which lists **(3)** *three or four / eight or nine* things that you must write about. You **(4)** *must / don't have to* answer all these points in your message. You **(5)** *must / don't have to* explain things in your own words, so avoid just copying things from the notice or announcement. For the other task, you are given the first **(6)** *paragraph / sentence* and you must continue it. You **(7)** *must / mustn't* try to do both tasks! If your answer is too short, you may get a **(8)** *higher / lower* mark for the task.

 **Listening Part 1**

Read the information about Listening Part 1. Complete the information with the words in the box.

vocabulary	pictures	multiple-choice	people	mark	recordings	facts

In Preliminary Listening Part 1, you hear seven short **(1)** .... For each recording, there is one **(2)** .... question to answer, and there are three **(3)** .... , A, B and C. You choose the correct picture to answer the question. The information you must listen for is based on **(4)** .... that you hear in the recording. Sometimes you hear two **(5)** .... speaking, and sometimes you only hear one. All the words you hear are from the Preliminary **(6)** .... list. You receive one **(7)** .... for each correct answer.

 **Listening Part 2**

Read the sentences about Listening Part 2. Are the sentences TRUE or FALSE?

1. In Part 2, you may hear two speakers or you may just hear one. ....

2. Each recording is quite short, like in the recordings in Part 1. ....

3. There are six multiple-choice questions to answer. ....

4. For each question, there are four possible answers, A, B, C or D, for you to choose from. ....

5. There are also pictures to help you choose an answer. ....

6. There are two marks for each correct answer. ....

7. For some questions, two correct answers are possible. ....

 **Listening Part 3**

Read the sentences about Listening Part 3. Are the sentences TRUE or FALSE?

1. There are five gaps for you to complete in Part 3. ....

2. You hear one person speaking in this part. ....

3. You have to write a word or short phrase in each gap. ....

4. You should try to spell the missing words correctly. ....

5. You should try to write exactly the words you hear in the gaps. ....

6. You get one mark for every word you write in a gap. ....

   So, if you write two words, you get two marks. ....

7. Every sentence or note you read has a gap in it. ....

 **Listening Part 4**

Match 1–8 to a–h to make sentences about Listening Part 4.

1. You answer six

2. Each question has

3. You hear

4. Sometimes you have to decide

5. To give your answers, you have to

6. Only one option for each question

7. You have to listen for the speakers'

8. You get

a three possible answers.

b what the interviewee's opinion is.

c choose either A, B or C.

d is correct.

e questions in this part of the test.

f an interview with someone.

g one mark for each correct answer.

h opinions and attitudes.

 **Speaking Part 1**

Read the sentences about Speaking Part 1. Are the sentences TRUE or FALSE?

1. You should talk to your partner during this part of the test. ....

2. You should give one-word answers. ....

3. The examiner may ask you questions about where you're from and what you do. ....

4. There are two phases to this part of the test. ....

5. You should ask your partner some questions about him / herself. ....

6. It's a good idea to practise answering personal questions before this part of the test. ....

7. If you don't understand a question, you can ask the examiner to repeat it. ....

8. The examiner will ask you some general questions, such as what you like doing in your free time, or what you enjoy about studying English. ....

 **Speaking Part 2**

Match 1–8 to a–h to make sentences about Speaking Part 2.

1. In Part 2, you have to describe

2. You will see a

3. You should describe everything

4. You should not talk

5. If there's something you don't know the word for,

6. Don't stop talking

7. Don't worry about making

8. Try not to compare yourself with your partner –

a you can see in the picture.

b describe it using other words.

c until the examiner asks you to.

d about things or ideas which are not in the picture.

e a picture.

f the examiner assesses each of you individually.

g different picture from your partner.

h mistakes – just keep talking!

 **Think about it** Speaking Part 3

Read the information about Speaking Part 3. Complete the information with the words in the box.

| partner | opportunity | situation | interested | opinions | stop | ask | pictures |

In Part 3, the examiner will describe a **(1)** .... to you and your **(2)** .... You should listen carefully to make sure you understand what the examiner says. The examiner will ask you to look at some **(3)** .... The examiner will then **(4)** .... you to talk about the situation. Then, you have to talk to your partner. Don't forget to ask for his or her **(5)** .... Remember to listen to what your partner says, and show that you are **(6)** .... in what they have to say. Make sure you give your partner enough **(7)** .... to speak, and interrupt politely if he / she talks too much. You should keep talking until the examiner asks you to **(8)** ....

 **Think about it** Speaking Part 4

Complete each sentence about Speaking Part 4 by choosing the correct option.

1. In Part 4, you talk about

a the same topic as Part 3.

b the same topic as Part 2.

2. During Part 4, the examiner will ask questions to

a you, or you and your partner.

b you or your partner separately.

3. You should

a ask your partner questions.

b wait for the examiner to ask you questions.

4. If you aren't sure what to say next, you could

a ask your partner for their opinion.

b ask the examiner what to do.

5. It's important to show that

a you know more than your partner about the topic.

b you are listening to what your partner is saying.

6. You should make sure that you

a talk as much as possible.

b give your partner a chance to speak.

7. Remember to

a talk about everything the examiner asks you to talk about.

b give answers that are as short and simple as possible.

8. You should try not to

a ask the examiner to repeat the instructions.

b sit in silence. If you need to, ask the examiner to repeat the instructions.

EXAM TOPIC LISTS

Clothes and Accessories

backpack
bag
belt
blouse
boot
bracelet
button
cap
chain
clothes
coat
collar
cotton
dress
earring
fashion
fasten
fit **(v)**
fold **(v)**
get dressed
glasses
glove

go (with/together)
(phr v)
handbag
handkerchief
hat
jacket
jeans
jewellery / jewelry
jumper
kit
knit
label
laundry
leather
make-up
match **(v)**
material
necklace
old-fashioned **(adj)**
pants
pattern

perfume
plastic
pocket
pullover
purse
put on
raincoat
ring
sandal
scarf
shirt
shoe
shorts
silk
size
skirt
sleeve(less)
socks
stripe
suit
sunglasses

sweater
swimming costume
swimsuit
take off
tie
tights
tracksuit
trainers
trousers
T-shirt
try on
umbrella
underpants
underwear
undress
uniform
wallet
watch
wear (out)
wool(len)

Colours

(dark/light/pale)
black
blue
brown

gold
golden
green
grey

orange
pink
purple
red

silver
yellow
white

Communications and Technology

access
address
app
at!@
blog
blogger
by post
calculator
call **(v)**
call back
CD (player)
cell phone
chat
chat room
click **(v)**
computer
connect
connection
data
delete
dial
dial up
digital
digital camera

disc/disk
dot
download **(n & v)**
drag
DVD (player)
electronic(s)
email
engaged
enter
envelope
equipment
fax
file
hang up
hardware
headline
homepage
install
internet
invent
invention
IT
keyboard
laptop (computer)

machine
message
mobile phone
mouse
mouse mat
MP3 player
net
online
operator
parcel
password
PC
phone
photograph
photography
podcast
postcard
print
printer
program(me)
reply
ring
ring up
robot

screen
server
sign up
smartphone
social media
software
switch off
switch on
talk
telephone
text
text message
turn off
turn on
upload **(n & v)**
video clip
volume
web
web page
website

Education

absent
advanced
arithmetic
art
beginner
bell
biology
blackboard

board
book
bookshelf
break up
break(time)
certificate
chemistry
class

classroom
clever
coach
college
composition
course
curriculum
degree

desk
dictionary
diploma
drama
economics
elementary
essay
geography

handwriting
history
homework
information
instructions
instructor
intermediate
IT
know
laboratory (lab)
language
learn
lesson

level
library
mark
math(s)
mathematics
music
nature studies
note
notice board
pencil case
photography
physics
practice (n)

practise (v)
primary school
project
pupil
qualification
read
register
remember
research
rubber
ruler
school
science

secondary school
student
studies
study (v)
subject
teach
teacher
technology
term
test
university

Entertainment and Media

act (v)
action
actor
actress
ad
admission
adventure
advert
advertisement
app
art
article
audience
ballet
band
bestseller
board game
book
camera
card
cartoon
CD (player)
CD-ROM
celebrity
channel
chat show
chess
cinema
circus

classical music
comedy
comic
competition
concert
dance
dancer
disc
disco
display
DJ / disc jockey
documentary
drama
draw
drawing
DVD (player)
entrance
exhibition
exit
festival
film
film maker
film star
fireworks
folk music
fun
go out
group
guitar

guitarist
headline
headphones
hero
heroine
hip hop
hit song
horror
instrument
interval
interview(er)
jazz music
journalist
keyboard
laugh
listen to
look at
magazine
magic
MP3 player
museum
music
musician
news
newspaper
opera
orchestra
paint
painter

perform
performance
performer
play
podcast
poem
pop music
presenter
production
programme
quiz
recording
review
rock music
romantic
row
scene
screen
selfie
series
soap opera
soundtrack
stage
star
studio
talk show
television
thriller
video

Environment

bottle bank
climate change
gas (Am Eng)
litter

petrol (Br Eng)
pollution
prohibited
public transport

recycle
recycled
recycling
rubbish (bin)

traffic jam
volunteer (n)

Food and Drink

apple
bake (v)
banana
barbecue (n & v)
bean
biscuit
bitter (adj)
boil (v)
boiled
bottle
bowl
box
bread
break

breakfast
broccoli
bunch (of bananas)
burger
butter
cabbage
cafe
cafeteria
cake
can (of beans)
candy
canteen
carrot
cereal

cheese
chef
chicken
chilli
chips
chocolate
coconut
coffee
cola
cook (n & v)
cooker
cookie
corn
cream

cucumber
cup
curry
cut
delicious
dessert
diet
dinner
dish
drink
duck
eat
egg
fish

flavour
flour
food
fork
French fries
fresh
fridge
fried
fruit
fruit juice
fry
frying pan
garlic
glass
grape
grill (n & v)
grilled
herbs
honey
hot
hungry
ice
ice cream
ingredients
jam
jug

juice
kitchen
knife
lamb
lemon
lemonade
lettuce
lunch
main course
meal
meat
melon
menu
microwave (n)
milk
mineral water
mushroom
oil
omelette
onion
orange
pan
pasta
pea
peach
peanut

pear
pepper
picnic
pie
piece of cake
pineapple
pizza
plate
potato
recipe
refreshments
rice
roast (v & adj)
roll
salad
salmon
salt
sandwich
sauce
saucepan
saucer
sausage
slice (n)
snack
soft drink
soup

sour
spicy
spinach
spoon
steak
strawberry
sugar
sweet (adj & n)
takeaway
taste
tasty
tea
thirsty
toast
tomato
tuna
turkey
vegetable
vegetarian
waiter
waitress
wash up
yog(h)urt

Health, Medicine and Exercise

accident
ache
ambulance
ankle
appointment
arm
aspirin
baby
bandage
bleed (v)
blood (n)
body
bone
brain
break
breath
breathe
check
chemist
chin
clean
cold (n)
comb
cough (n & v)
cut
damage

danger
dangerous
dead
dentist
die
diet
doctor
ear
earache
emergency
exercise
eye
face
fall
feel better/ill/sick
fever
finger
fit
flu
foot
get better/worse
go jogging
gym
gymnastics
hair
hand

head
headache
health
hear
heart
heel
hospital
hurt
ill
illness
injure
keep fit
knee
leg
lie down
medicine
nose
nurse
operate
operation
pain
painful
patient (n)
pharmacy
pill
prescription

problem
recover
rest (n & v)
run
shoulder
sick
skin
soap
sore throat
stomach
stomach ache
stress
swim
tablet
take exercise
temperature
thumb
tired
toes
tooth
toothache
toothbrush
walk
well (adj)

Hobbies and Leisure

barbecue
beach
bicycle
bike
camera
camp
camping
campsite
CD (player)
chess

club
collect(or)
collection
computer
cruise
dance
dancing
doll
draw
drawing

DVD (player)
facilities
fan
festival
fiction
gallery
go out
go shopping
guitar
hang out

hike
hire
hobby
holidays
ice skates
jogging
join in
keen on
keep fit
magazine

member(ship)	opening	photograph	sightseeing
model	hours	picnic	slide
museum	paint	playground	sunbathe
music	painting	quiz	tent
musician	park	rope	torch
nightlife	party	sculpture	

House and Home

accommodation	computer	heater	remote control
address	cooker	heating	rent
air conditioning	cottage	hi-fi	repair
alarm (fire/car)	cupboard	home	roof
alarm clock	curtain	house	room
antique	cushion	housewife	roommate
apartment	desk	housework	rubbish
armchair	digital (adj)	iron	safe (adj)
balcony	dining room	jug	seat
basin	dish	kettle	sheet
bath (tub)	dishwasher	key	shelf
bathroom	door	kitchen	shower
bed	downstairs	ladder	sink
bedroom	drawer	lamp	sitting room
bell	dustbin	laptop (computer)	sofa
bin	duvet	lift	stairs
blanket	DVD (player)	light	stay (v)
blind	electric(al)	(clothes) line	step
block	entrance	living-room	surround
(notice) board	fan	lock	switch
bookcase	flat	microwave (n)	table
bookshelf	flatmate	mirror	tap
bowl	floor	mug	telephone
box	freezer	neighbour	television
brush	fridge	oil	toilet
bucket	frying pan	oven	towel
bulb	furniture	pan	tower
candle	garage	path	toy
carpet	garden	pillow	TV (screen/set)
ceiling	gas	pipe	upstairs (adv)
cellar	gate	plant	vase
central heating	grill	plug	video
chair	ground (floor)	plug in	wall
channel (with TV)	hall	property	washing machine
chest of drawers	handle	radio	window
clock	heat (v)	refrigerator	

Language

advanced	elementary	mention	speak
answer	email	message	talk
argue	grammar	pronounce	tell
ask	intermediate	pronunciation	translate
beginner	joke	question	translation
chat	letter	say	vocabulary
communicate	mean	sentence	word
communication	meaning	shout	

Personal Feelings, Opinions and Experiences (Adjectives)

able	awesome	busy	confusing
afraid	awful	calm	cool
alone	bad	careful	crazy
amazed	beautiful	challenging	cruel
amazing	better	charming	curious
amusing	bored	cheerful	cute
angry	boring	clear	delighted
annoyed	bossy	clever	depressed
anxious	brave	confident	different
ashamed	brilliant	confused	difficult

disappointed	happy	old	slow
disappointing	hard	old-fashioned	small
easy	healthy	ordinary	smart
embarrassed	heavy	original	soft
embarrassing	high	patient	sorry
enjoyable	hungry	personal	special
excellent	important	pleasant	strange
excited	impressed	poor	strong
exciting	intelligent	positive	stupid
famous	interested	pretty	sure
fantastic	interesting	quick	surprised
favourite	jealous	quiet	sweet
fine	keen	ready	tall
fit	kind	real	terrible
fond	lazy	realistic	tired
free	lovely	reasonable	true
friendly	lucky	relaxed	typical
frightened	mad	reliable	unable
frightening	married	relieved	unhappy
funny	miserable	rich	unusual
generous	modern	right	useful
gentle	negative	rude	well
glad	nervous	sad	wonderful
good	nice	satisfied	worried
great	noisy	serious	wrong
guilty	normal	slim	young

Places: Buildings

apartment block /	college	hospital	railway station
apartment	cottage	hotel	ruin
building	department store	house	school
bank	disco	library	shop
bookshop	elevator	lift	sports centre
bookstore	entrance	mall (shopping)	stadium
building	exit	museum	supermarket
café	factory	office	swimming pool
cafeteria	flat	palace	theatre
castle	gallery	police station	tourist
cinema	garage	pool	information centre
clinic	grocery store	post office	tower
club	guest-house	prison	university

Places: Countryside

area	field	path	sea
bay	forest	port	seaside
beach	harbour	railway	sky
campsite	hill	rainforest	stream
canal	island	region	valley
cliff	lake	river	village
desert	land	rock	waterfall
earth	mountain	sand	wood
farm	ocean	scenery	

Places: Town and City

apartment	cashpoint	park	square
building	city centre	pavement	station
airport	corner	petrol station	street
booking office	crossing	playground	subway
bridge	crossroads	road	town
bus station	fountain	roundabout	tunnel
bus stop	market	route	turning
car park	motorway	shopping centre	underground
cash machine	monument	(shopping) mall	zoo
		signpost	

Services

bank	doctor	library	swimming pool
café	gallery	museum	theatre
cafeteria	garage	post office	tourist information
cinema	hairdresser	restaurant	
dentist	hotel	sports centre	

Shopping

ad	close (v)	for sale	receipt
advert	closed	go shopping	reduce
advertise	collect	hire	reduced
advertisement	complain	inexpensive	rent
assistant	cost (n & v)	label	reserve
bargain	credit card	logo	return
bill	customer	luxury	save
book	damaged	mall	second-hand
buy	dear	money	sell
cash	department store	order	shop
cent	deposit	pay (for)	shop assistant
change	dollar	penny	shopper
cheap	euro	pound	shopping
cheque	exchange	price	spend
choose	expensive	reasonable	supermarket
			try on

Sport

athlete	extreme sports	net	sport(s)
athletics	(sports) facilities	pitch (n)	sports centre
badminton	fishing	play (v)	squash
ball	fitness	point(s)	stadium
baseball	football	practice (n)	surf
basketball	football player	practise (v)	surfboard
bat	game	prize	surfboarding
bathing suit	goal	race	surfing
beach	goalkeeper	race track	swim
bicycle	golf	racing	swimming
bike	gym	racket	swimming costume
boat	gymnastics	reserve (n)	swimming pool
boxing	helmet	rest (n & v)	swimsuit
catch (v)	high jump	ride (n & v)	table tennis
champion	hit (v)	rider	take part
championship	hockey	riding	team
changing room	horse-riding	rugby	tennis
climb (v)	ice hockey	run (n & v)	tennis player
climbing	ice skates	running	throw (v)
club	ice skating	sail (n & v)	ticket
coach (n)	instructor	sailing	tired
compete	jogging	score	track
competition	join in	sea	tracksuit
competitor	kick (v)	season	trainer(s)
contest	kit	shoot(ing)	train(ing)
court	league	shorts	versus / v.
cricket	locker (room)	skateboard	volleyball
cycling	long jump	skating	walk (v)
cyclist	luck	skiing	watch (v)
dancing	match	snowboard	water skiing
diving	member	snowboarding	win
enter (a competition)	motor-racing	soccer	workout
			yoga

The Natural World

air	branch	coast	donkey
animal	bush	continent	duck
autumn	butterfly	country	earth
beach	cave	countryside	east
bee	cliff	desert	elephant
bird	climate	dolphin	environment

environmental
explore(r)
fall **(Am Eng)**
farmland
field
fire
fish
flood
flower
forest
freeze
frog
fur
giraffe
grass
grow
hill
hot
ice

island
jungle
kangaroo
lake
land
leaf
lion
monkey
moon
mosquito
mountain
mouse / mice
nature
north
parrot
penguin
planet
plant
pollution

rabbit
rainforest
range
river
rock
sand
scenery
sea
shark
sky
south
space
species
spring
star
stone
summer
sun
sunrise

sunset
sunshine
tiger
tree
valley
water
waterfall
waves
west
wild
wildlife
winter
wood
wool
world
zebra

Time

afternoon
a.m. / p.m.
ages (for ages)
appointment
approximately
autumn
birthday
century
clock
daily
date
diary

evening
half (past)
holidays
hour
January – December
meeting
midnight
minute
moment
Monday – Sunday
month

monthly
morning
night
noon
o'clock
past
quarter (past / to)
second
spring
summer
time

today
tomorrow
tonight
week
weekday
weekend
weekly
winter
working hours
year
yesterday

Travel and Transport

abroad
accommodation
(aero)/(air)plane
airline
airport
ambulance
announcement
arrival
arrive
astronaut
at sea
backpack
backpacker
backpacking
bag
baggage
bicycle / bike
board **(v)**
boarding pass
boat
border
bridge
brochure
bus
bus station
bus stop
by air
by land
by rail
by road
by sea

cab
cabin
canal
capital city
car
car alarm
car park
case
catch **(v)**
change **(v)**
charter
check in **(v)**
check-in **(n)**
check out **(v)**
coach
confirm
country
crossing
crossroads
currency
customs
cycle **(n & v)**
cyclist
delay
delayed
deliver
depart
departure
destination
direction
document(s)

dollar
double room
drive
driver
driving/driver's licence
due
duty-free
embassy
euro
exchange rate
facilities
far
fare
ferry
flight
fly
foreign
fuel
garage
gas / gas station
   (Am Eng)
gate
guest
guide
guidebook
handlebars
harbour
helicopter
hitchhike
hotel
immigration

jet
journey
land **(v)**
leave
left
light
lorry
luggage
machine
map
mechanic
mirror
miss
motorbike
motorway
move
nationality
oil
on board
on business
on foot
on holiday
on time
on vacation
operator
overnight
park **(v)**
parking lot
parking space
passenger
passport

path
petrol
petrol station
pilot
platform public
transport
railroad
railway
reception
repair **(v)**
reservation
reserve
return **(n & v)**
ride
road sign

rocket
roundabout
route
sail **(v)**
scooter
(bus) service
ship
sightseeing
signpost
single room
spaceship
speed
subway
suitcase
take off

taxi
tour **(n & v)**
tour guide
tourist
tourist information centre
traffic
traffic jam
traffic lights
train
tram
translate
translation
travel
trip
tunnel

tyre/tire
underground
underground train
vehicle
visa
visit(or)
waiting room
way
wheel
window
windscreen

Weather

blow
breeze
cloud
cloudy
cold
cool
degrees
dry
fog
foggy

forecast
freezing
frozen
gale
get wet
heat
hot
humid
ice
icy

lightning
mild
rain
shower
snow
snowfall
storm
sun
sunny
sunshine

temperature
thunder(storm)
warm
weather
wet
wind
windy

Work and Jobs

actor
actress
application
apply
architect
army
artist
assistant
astronaut
athlete
babysitter
banker
barber
boss
break **(n)**
businessman
businesswoman
butcher
cameraman
candidate
canteen
captain
career
chef
chemist
cleaner
colleague
company
computer
conference
contract
cook
crew
customs officer
CV
dancer
dentist

department
designer
desk
detective
diary
diploma
director
diver
doctor
earn
email
employ **(v)**
employee
employer
employment
engineer
explorer
factory
farm
farmer
film star
firefighter
football player / footballer
full time
goalkeeper
guard
guest
guide
hairdresser
housewife
housework
instructions
instructor
job
journalist
judge
king

laboratory
lawyer
lecturer
letter
librarian
manager
mechanic
meeting
message
model
musician
novelist
nurse
occupation
office
officer (e.g. prison/police)
out of work
owner
painter
part time
photographer
pilot
poet
policeman
police officer
policewoman
politician
porter
postman
president
profession
professional
professor
(computer) programmer
publisher
qualification
queen

quit
receptionist
reporter
retire
retirement
sailor
salary
sales assistant
salesman
saleswoman
scientist
secretary
security guard
shop assistant
shopper
singer
soldier
staff
student
taxi driver
teacher
tennis player
tour guide
trade
travel agent
unemployed
uniform
volunteer **(n)**
wage(s)
waiter / waitress
work
worker

ACKNOWLEDGEMENTS

The authors and publishers acknowledge the following sources of copyright material and are grateful for the permissions granted. While every effort has been made, it has not always been possible to identify the sources of all the material used, or to trace all copyright holders. If any omissions are brought to our notice, we will be happy to include the appropriate acknowledgements on reprinting and in the next update to the digital edition, as applicable.

Keys: R = Reading, L = Listening, W = Writing, S = Speaking, P = Part

Photography

All the images are sourced from Getty Images.

RP1: ScottTalent/DigitalVision Vectors; David Lees/Taxi; zacky24/iStock/Getty Images plus; Paolo Cordelli/Lonely Planet Images; **RP2**: Michael Blann/Stone; Neil Beckerman/Taxi; Design Pics; Dave and Les Jacobs/Kolostock/Blend Images; Ogphoto/E+; Vesna Andjic/E+; moodboard/Brand X Pictures; David Schaffer/Caiaimage; Justin Case/DigitalVision; Jacqueline Veissid/DigitalVision; Dougal Waters/DigitalVision; Mike Harrington/The Image Bank; Peter Rutherhagen; Lane Oatey/Blue Jean Images; **RP3**: monkeybusinessimages/iStock/Getty Images plus; **RP4**: Andrew Yates/AFP; The Washington Post; UpperCut Images; Danita Delimont/Gallo Images/Getty Images Plus; Deb Alperin/Moment; **RP5**: Isa Foltin/WireImage; Francois Guillot/AFP; Eastcott Momatiuk/The Image Bank; RP6: martinedoucet/E+; sturti/E+; imagenavi; AntonioGuillem/iStock/Getty Images Plus; Fuse/Corbis; vgajic/E+; **WP1**: Marvin E. Newman/Photographer's Choice; Marion Nesje/Moment; **WP2**: andresr/E+; Steve Sands/Getty Images Entertainment; Hill Street Studios LLC/DigitalVision; Stephen Simpson/Iconica; Mohamed Abdulla Shafeeg/Moment; **LP2**: DAJ; John Fedele; skynesher/E+; **LP3**: filadendron/E+; Erik Von Weber/The Image Bank; zoranm/iStock/Getty Images Plus; Ryan McVay/DigitalVision; SolStock/E+; **LP4**: Ezra Bailey/Iconica; Jekaterina Nikitina/Stone; Flashpop/DigitalVision; Jacek Chabraszewski/iStock/Getty Images plus; Dennis Fischer Photography/Moment; **SP1**: Juanmonino/E+; Westend61; skynesher/E+; **SP2**: Oli Scarff/Getty Images News; Brent Winebrenner/Lonely Planet Images; Sarma Ozols/The Image Bank; Tom Fletcher/EyeEm; Ursula Alter/Photographer's Choice; Charlie Drevstam; Nadine Funke/EyeEm; bortonia/DigitalVision Vectors; Charlie Abad/Photononstops; Rob Stothard/Getty Images News; Xavier Arnau/E+; Giordano Poloni/Ikon Images; KidStock/Blend Images; Hero Images; **SP3**: kali9/E+.

Illustrations

Daniel Limon; QBS.

Audio production by Hart McLeod, Cambridge and by DN and AE Strauss Ltd. Cambridge.